A CHILD CRIES

"No-one can see my tears
because they are inside,
deep inside,
and they hurt."

— A Child's Thoughts

A special limited edition

First published in Great Britain in 2003
"A Child Cries"
'Downwood', Bath, BA26DT.
A C.I.P. catalogue record for this book is available
from the British Library.

Designed by Steve Carroll
Edited by Jill Gupta
Illustrations by Annabelle Hicks
Photographs © Mirrorpix
Printed in India
ISBN 086347 5914

"The Slums, the children's
homes. Now 'home'.
All strange places to live.
I wonder what next."
—— A Child's Thoughts

CONTENTS

By Way of Introduction

Opening my memory banks to my first fifteen years of life has been an emotional 'roller coaster' as I have revisited a life that no child should have to live.

My first few years were spent in the over-crowded squalor of an inner-city slum as well as times in large Institutions for children in need.

My first fifteen years were...

...years of becoming a stranger to my own family.

...years of becoming 'invisible' to my mother who eventually deserted me and my siblings. We did not hear from her for nearly twenty-eight years.

...years of being an object of cruel and violent abuse by my father.

...years of having my thoughts trapped in my mind

"The family I came into was not a happy one.
Bombs were falling.
Mother absent.
Father drunk.
Siblings scattered.
Slums smelly.
Food scarce.
Water dirty.
Toilets unusable.
Speech trapped.
The world mad.
Love lost.

Me? .... A Waste.

Sorry, so, so, sorry!"

— A Child's Thoughts

because dyslexia and an inability to speak clearly due to a physical defect that restricted the movement of my tongue.

...years uneducated and unnoticed at school, unloved and unwanted by parents, left to run wild away from shame and pain into an ever decreasing tunnel of becoming 'nobody' with nothing to look forward to.

> "The way for me to overcome not being able to read is page by page and word by word even if it takes years to do it"
>
> — A Child's Thoughts

...years that dragged on until I drew blood in a fight for my survival and for my destiny as a human being.

In writing my story, I have been rediscovering my childhood family and have experienced an affection impossible to describe. Without their experiences and memories, alongside my own, this story would have been much the poorer.

"A Child Cries" is written against the background of the Second World War and the changing world that followed it. I have tried to reflect both in the story.

I have concluded my story with an Historical Supplement: a romantic tale contrasting two villages, which I wrote for the citizens of Birmingham and of my own lost village of Bartley Green, although I hope all readers will find it interesting.

Following the first fifteen years covered in this

story, it took another fifteen years before I felt confident enough to launch out and fulfil my own dreams... but that's another story!

ACKNOWLEDGMENTS

My acknowledgments are in chronological order.

To my first wife Joyce, now in Heaven, who spent many early years of our marriage supporting me as I attemted to overcome the multiple defects in my character and conduct, as well as helping me to read and write and gain confidence in my own abilities, and who gave me four lovely children who now with their spouses have given me fourteen happy grandchildren.

To Gilbert Kirby, a retired Principal of a London College, who encouraged me fifteen years ago to write my story, believing it would be an inspiration and motivation to others. Having planted the seed in my mind, over the years the idea has grown.

> "All my life, I have been robbed.
> But no more."
> — A Child's Thoughts

To Esther Rantzen, whose personal words to me have pushed me into actual writing. I was a guest on her popular BBC show, *Esther*, after which she briefly spoke to me while shooting a 'commercial' for her show. She simply said, "Your story is a book..." As Esther Rantzen has interviewed numerous people over the years, I trusted her evaluation and found myself writing.

To my two elder siblings, John and Jean and my two younger brothers Bernard and Brian, I am deeply indebted, not only for the fresh discovery of affection between us, but also for sharpening my memory banks in our recent happy times together.*

> "Maybe, one day, I will have someone to help me. Maybe, one day, I will have a friend... but I am not sure. Maybe's are only dreams."
> — A Child's Thoughts

To my wife Annabelle, not only for her understanding and encouragement, but also for typing, correcting and retyping the manuscript, a laborious job because I do not relate to modern technology and need a 'hands-on' helper.

Last, and definitely not least, to our grown-up eight-year-old daughter Emily-Rose whose spontaneous happiness is in such contrast to her father's experiences at that age, but who in a miraculous way is also a compensation for it.

---

* Only two names in the book have been changed for sensitive reasons.

DEDICATION

To Donald, my half-brother, now in Heaven.

To John my older brother, whom I now realise protected us all from many severe beatings when he was at home with us.

To Jean, my sister, who suffered more than all of us, and whom I have learned to love and admire with brotherly affection.

To my younger brother Bernard, who like myself felt a stranger in his own family.

To Brian the youngest of us all at home who should never have had to suffer the way he did.

To Tracey, my half-sister, and any other half-sisters or half-brothers whom I have never met, but perhaps one day will, maybe even as a result of writing this story.

To the children of Stonehouse Lane who were there in those ten years 1946-1956.

And to the N.S.P.C.C. – a Children's Charity for which I am most grateful.

> "My head is full, my heart is heavy, my speech is wrong, my home is cold, my life is empty. That's me in a nutshell."
>
> — A Child's Thoughts

"The children are always playing; they have escaped the slums. But Mom and Dad are always wanting to go back to the city. I don't understand it."

FEBRUARY 26TH

STAINED WITH BLOOD

One o'clock in the morning, 26 February, 1956.

It was cold – an unnatural, penetrating chill, not caused by the elements of weather.

All the lights were out in the long row of terraced houses in Stonehouse Lane, Bartley Green. It was a very quiet place, being some twelve miles from the bright lights and nightlife of Birmingham, that great, modern industrial city.

> "Can I do it?
> Should I do it?
> Will I do it?
> What will happen?
>
> But I must, I must, I must.
> Yet it's not natural or fair
> ... but I must!"
>
> — A Child's Thoughts

The last bus from the city centre had long since gone. It was my fifteenth birthday, but that was of no consequence. This anniversary would pass by – like all other birthdays – unnoticed by anyone, including myself.

My short-sleeved bright yellow shirt was spattered with the blood that had also spurted onto my face. I could feel the droplets trickling towards my mouth.

3

Instinctively, I tried to stop them, willing my tongue to remove the sticky sensation that filled me with nausea.

I failed, because my tongue was fixed to the base of my mouth, a defect I had endured from birth and one that caused me to be the subject of ridicule, and thought of as an idiot, especially as I also suffered from dyslexia – a cross-wiring in my brain!

The blood on my pale face and yellow shirt was my father's.

I had drawn that blood from him in the narrow kitchen of our house, the same kitchen in which his young children had been so cruelly robbed of the best of their childhood, psychologically damaged, and chained to immense obstacles for the rest of their lives.

> "They do not understand what I am saying. I cannot say what they want me to.
> I am not the same as other children.
> If only I could speak the way they want me to!"
>
> — A Child's Thoughts

It was here, in this house, next door to Hell itself, where my natural inclination to be a bright happy child had been cruelly redirected, turning me into a sad loner, sinking deeper and deeper into myself.

I would dream of this nightmare scene in the kitchen again and again, but in my dreams I would be a spectator, holding my breath lest the boy should lose his nerve or miss his cue. At the height of the drama, my thumping heart would beat more loudly. My attention would be riveted on a young boy in a bright yellow nylon shirt and on the blood which ran down the front of his shirt making crazy patterns on the shiny material.

I had been building up to this moment for ages. In a few weeks' time I would be leaving school. I would have to survive without its protection and without the free hot meals served there every day in the week. I would have to face the great unknown – with nothing. I was a nobody, unloved, unwanted, unacknowledged, not belonging to anyone or anything. Before me was a vast alien world which I knew I was ill-equipped to face. My tomorrow was dark, with no perceivable light, and I knew I would have to take control of my own life and destiny if I was to survive.

If anyone else had been in that narrow kitchen at that moment, they would have recoiled from the stench. The smell of recently fried, greasy bacon would have assaulted the senses mingled as it was with the reek of cheap tobacco smoke, stale beer, weak tea and the rank odour of fear.

A witness to the scene would have noticed a change taking place. Dad's voice altered. He was breathing faster as the tension between us increased. His eyes became glazed and wild as he spat out false accusations

and violent threats. Although Dad seldom looked me straight in the face, as a child I was always aware of his eyes. When I saw them fill with anger and his own internal pain I knew he would take it out on me. His body tensed and his fingers moved rapidly, like a boxer flexing his muscles before a fight. Slowly he squeezed his hands until his knuckles went white. My usual reaction would have been to edge my way to the corner of the ill-fitted back door, where the cold draught would send a shiver through me, and prepare to drop down into a curled-up position to protect myself from the imminent violence. But this time I knew I had to hit him before he hit me. I had to land a punch with all the force I could muster into his protruding belly, for he was no longer as fit as he had been a few years ago. I knew I would have to hit him with every ounce of muscle in my body – and I was small for my age.

I had acted out what I would do next many times. As his head came down, and before he could get his breath back, my knee would go up to make contact with his jaw and hopefully knock him out. I had not planned anything beyond that. I had only determined, 'I must fight! I must fight! I must fight!' so that he would no longer believe that I was the passive object of his cruel bullying wrath. I was fighting for my future, not my past, even though I had every reason to fight for that. The verbal intimidation, accusations and threats were over. It would be now or never.

As I waited, I noticed the objects around us. The ragged-edged carving knife, used to saw a large chunk of bread from the loaf, was in easy reach, as was a saucepan of boiling water left over from making the tea, and a frying pan in which the greasy bacon had been cooked.

The narrow kitchen was the warmest part of the house at this time of the night, yet the atmosphere was cold. That dreadful smell of fear seemed to cling to the walls and ceiling.

> "I will do it! I will; I must! I can be 'somebody'."
> — A Child's Thoughts

I was all too conscious of the voice, the eyes, the muscles in his body, and the white of his knuckles. He moved towards me. All my senses co-ordinated and an invisible force propelled me to do something that was not natural to me. Even as I prepared to make my move, everything in my head told me I was acting out of character.

In front of me stood a big strong man who should have been my 'father', my mentor, my friend, a person who was interested in my future and what I would do with my life.

Instead there was a monster who was about to do

7

what he had done so many times before. Something inside me snapped. This was my fight for my freedom. I accepted the fact that I was nothing – not only to others, but also to myself. I would remain nothing, unless I fought back. Being nothing was worse than being nobody. All my life I had been nobody, not even a son to my father or my mother.

It was now or never! I knew it, I knew it! Now or never!

I hit him first with all the resolve I could muster, energised by a spring that had been wound up tighter and tighter within me over a long period of time. My small curled-up fist sank into his belly, completely winding him. Just as I had practised many times, my knee began to move upwards to make contact with his chin. He was bent over with pain and his head dropped forward. In that fraction of a second before my knee hit him on the chin, he looked up and for the first time that I can remember, our eyes locked. I saw in his eyes the same fear that we children had felt so many times. His expression mirrored that of Lassie our dog after he had beaten him, his eyes wide open in bewilderment and fear as he looked into his master's face, pleading for

> "I don't like the kitchen at night. It is the worst place in all the world. It is cold and I am all alone with Dad. I am afraid."
> — A Child's Thoughts

mercy. Sometimes you can look into a person's eyes and see his soul. As our eyes met, and before my knee felt the shudder of contact, I saw into his soul and I knew that I had won! The evil spell he had held over me for many years was broken. For the first time in my young life of terror, I was free!

You could hear the crack, like the sound of a whiplash, in that kitchen of dark secrets and monstrous deeds. My knee hit Dad's chin as his body fell towards me. The force pushed his head right back and he began to fall in the opposite direction towards the stove. The blood spurted out of his mouth, all over my face and my bright yellow shirt. That shirt was the only item of clothing my father had ever bought me. It was stolen property, acquired by him in exchange for a pint of beer in the pub. Now his one and only gift to me was stained with his own red blood.

He had bitten his tongue and his teeth had cut open his bottom lip. The impact had loosened two of his teeth and he had lost one of them.

I was not expecting blood and I was frightened by the gruesome sight. He had slumped to his knees and he was gasping for breath, his neck and shoulders thrown back.

In that moment I caught sight of the bread knife. In years to come, I would have disturbing flashbacks

imagining how easy it would have been to have cut his throat there and then. Even though my sister and I had previously worked out a plan to kill Dad, thankfully, I wasn't tempted to do such a thing because I knew I had won! The wicked spell was broken. As I heard him groaning and saw the look in his eyes, my stomach heaved and I was sick, adding to the stench of this never-to-be-forgotten hour.

> "I think I should be happy. Something must be wrong."
> — A Child's Thoughts

This kitchen and, worse, Dad's bedroom, were a mirror reflection of Hell itself – so, so terrible – and although I had won my freedom and would never be afflicted physically again, I knew I was lost and alone, with nothing in the world and nowhere to go. I had been forced to fight for my sanity and my future; to fight against a man who, although biologically my father, had forfeited that relationship many times.

CHAPTER 1

A LONE BOMBER AND
A PREGNANT WOMAN

months' pregnant with her fourth child and was sleeping restlessly. She knew that the next morning she must gather together her few belongings and put them in the old pram with its buckled wheel and warped steering. Then she must look for new rooms in the Birmingham slums that had been condemned a hundred years earlier.

The pregnant woman was being evicted for not paying the rent. She had been evicted many times and the pattern would be repeated again and again over the next six years.

> "I was her fourth child but she never knew my birthday. She never knew me - not even for one day in a year."
>
> — A Child's Thoughts

When Great Britain and France declared war against Nazi Germany, Birmingham played its part in the nationwide evacuation of 1,500,000 souls from the city centres into the countryside. Of these, nearly 500,000 were pregnant women but this woman ignored the chance to evacuate, refusing to take herself or her children to safety. It was not only her strong will and belief that she was different which led her to reject the offer. She was also living a double life, one which did not include her children.

For those sent to the countryside, it was a first-time experience. Many of the poor folk from the cities

danced on the green grass and filled their lungs with the fresh air. They were overcome by their discovery of the countryside, something that they had never even known existed. One of these children wrote to his mother, 'They call this Spring, and they tell us it comes every year!'

By August 1940 a year had elapsed during which the dreaded bombings had not happened. It seemed to be a phoney war. Many of the women had returned with their newborn babies and children to their families in the cities. Even poor families preferred the community life of the slums to the condescending charity of some well-meant but insensitive country folk.

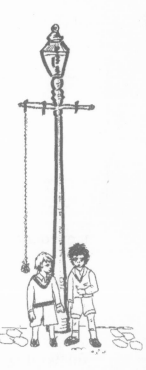

The noise of the German warplane's engine grew louder and louder. The prophecy of all that evil could bring was about to be fulfilled. For the first time warplanes flew immediately over the cities spitting out their destructive power. Thousands upon thousands would meet with a death more cruel than their worst nightmares. There was no escape.

In Erdington, five miles from the city centre, the lone bomber gave birth to his evil monsters. Having

ROBERT HICKS

dropped his cargo, he made his journey back to Germany, soon to return accompanied by his extended family of hundreds, making the sky even darker than at night. World War Two was now on everybody's doorstep.

The next morning, everyone was talking about the air raid. People started to carry their gasmasks wherever they went and they responded to the screaming sound of sirens with alacrity. The raid was a wake-up call for cities like Birmingham, targeted by Hitler and Goering for mass destruction.

> "I don't remember when I was very little but I know I was never allowed to be 'myself'. I was alone and unloved."
> — A Child's Thoughts

Making her way along the littered streets pushing her large old-fashioned wobbly pram was the twenty-two-year-old pregnant woman. She was going to her mother's house until she could find other rooms to rent.

That young woman was my mother. She was the firstborn of seven children. Her brothers and sisters were brought up in a cramped slum but mother was raised by her grandparents, an arrangement which protected her from the worst effect of the slums. In her teens they paid for her to receive a private education.

Yes, mother was different. She was attractive and

16

confident thanks to her special education, but trapped within her mother's culture – a culture she rebelled against vigorously. Distinctive, educated, yet flawed, for mother was attracted to physically handsome men, never bothering to discover their character, sense of purpose or motivation.

In the autumn of 1940 she tramped the streets looking for a home for herself, her three infants and the baby yet to be born. That baby was me, her fourth child.

After the lone German bomber, there were repeated missions by his companions dropping their murderous cargo. A few weeks later, on 25 October 1940, nineteen people were killed in Charlton Picture House in a place called Sparkbrook.

The following month 350 warplanes emptied their bowels over Birmingham. Thousands of houses were destroyed. In one air raid alone, 400 people met a violent and unexpected death. In one of these raids, mother's brother was found dead in a cellar. On the day of his burial, there were so many funerals taking place that the roads leading to the churches were choked with mourners.

During the 'blitz' over 2,200 'Brummies' – as they were called – would die, more than 3,000 would be

seriously wounded and 3,500 injured.

The Christmas of 1940 was a cold one. Death, by weapons of swift destruction, mingled with the sleet and snow. Proud landmarks were destroyed including the market place, the Music Hall, distinctive picture houses and the Prince of Wales Theatre but worst hit were the overcrowded areas of the city where the poor lived. As ever, the poor and innocent suffered most in the war. Over 100,000 homes became uninhabitable, leaving thousands of families bewildered, not knowing where they would sleep from one night to the next. Many had seen Atlantic City being consumed by fire in the film *Gone With the Wind*. They had gone to the picture houses for an hour or two of escapism but what they saw was a reflection of the destruction that was actually taking place in their own city.

> "I was told I had a baby sister, but I have never seen her. I want to see her and in a strange way I miss her very much."
> — A Child's Thoughts

On 26 February 1941 my mother was admitted to a private nursing home in Handsworth, having paid seven shillings and sixpence (35 pence) to have her three children looked after in a local Salvation Army Children's Hostel for the ten days of her confinement. It remains a mystery where the money came from.

The nursing home had been bombed and the

evidence of the bombing was everywhere. Windows were boarded up in some of the rooms and thick canvas sheeting was nailed across gaping holes in a vain attempt to protect the house from the elements. However, part of the house was functioning well enough for my mother to give birth to me on the afternoon of 26 February 1941, one of the coldest Februarys recorded in the twentieth century. Her first baby, Donald, was born in January 1938. His father was an Irish brickie. Mother claimed he was the only true love of her life and wasn't around only because he'd been wrongly imprisoned. John was born in December of that same year. To bring two babies into the world in the same year by two different men was a disgrace, even by the standards of the

slum mothers who had become little more than baby machines. Mother said that John was the result of her being raped by my father, whom she agreed to marry just two months before John arrived in order to cover up her shame. Jean was born twelve months later. She was the only girl in the family of six children. A seventh half-sister would be born later, but given up for adoption.

As the German war machine was in full flow and

> "The men sing loud songs and smell of beer, and then they are sick and the buckets come out week after week."
>
> — A Child's Thoughts

the bombs fell repeatedly on Birmingham and other cities nearby, chaos reigned.

The citizens of Birmingham – a million souls – were a mixture of different classes. Society in those days was divided into three classes, the upper, middle and lower-working class but, in Birmingham and other industrial cities, there was also a fourth class. This was made up of the lowest of the low, the poor people who lived in the squalor of the slums. Birmingham was growing wealthy and strong. Its motto, 'Forward' was apt but those who lived in the slums made little progress and had nothing to look forward to. Old black-and-white pictures do not adequately depict the dirt and squalor in which little children played games within the restricted courtyards that were their world. No image can convey the disgusting smells which assaulted the senses. They came from the toilets, each of which was shared by twenty or more people and which no amount of cheap disinfectant could disguise; from the local beer swilled down in vast quantities at weekends; from the hot fat used to fry fish and chips and greasy bacon and from the ubiquitous stewed tea. One of my earliest memories is of women carrying buckets of water on

Monday mornings trying to wash away the mess of human waste left by drunken men on the previous two nights.

My mother gave birth to me on the afternoon of Tuesday, 26 February 1941. I weighed 8 pounds and 4 ounces. All mother's children were heavy. I had the same soft creamy complexion as my grandmother, a fine head of hair and brown eyes. I was described at that time as having a naturally happy face. Understandably, mother was worn out. She had moved rooms time and again, had four children in less than three years, struggled through the Blitz, lost her brother and coped with one of the coldest winters of that century. With her three other children being looked after by the Salvation Army and with ten days of convalescence ahead of her, she gave way to exhaustion and fell into a deep sleep.

Usually a newborn baby was placed in a separate nursery but because part of the house had been destroyed in the recent bombing, I was put in another part of the same room where mother was now sleeping. Fast asleep, she did not hear the high-pitched siren. Everyone else in the nursing home, having been hit once, was on the alert and the home was vacated with great haste. Mother and I, however, were overlooked.

Whether it was the siren, the bombing, hunger or

21

the sound of her baby crying, eventually my mother awoke. Anyone hearing me cry would have realised it was not the normal sound a newborn baby makes. My tongue was tied to the base of my mouth by two mem-branes. This disability would hinder my progress in many ways over the next fifteen years before it was ultimately dealt with. Although that day I cried and cried, I soon discovered that nothing was gained from crying and, in the end, I learnt to cry inwardly so no one could hear any sound or see any tears. Babies express themselves by crying. It is their only defence mechanism against their need for food, comfort and the physical presence of love. The Hicks' children were not born into that kind of environment. Crying was pointless. It elicited no response. We learnt that lesson very early.

> "Jesus had a manger,
> I had a cardboard box.
> I am glad Jesus wasn't
> born in a palace."
> — A Child's Thoughts

When mother realised that we had both been left behind she abandoned me and went to look for someone to help her. She thought nothing of leaving her hours-old baby alone while she tried to find a way out. If this response to the situation revealed a lack of certain basic maternal instincts, then this was confirmed by her abandonment of all her children to her husband, knowing that he was a cruel and violent

man who became even more brutal and vicious under the influence of alcohol.

Eventually, she came across an old man who acted as the home's caretaker. He had stayed in the building, undeterred by the danger for he had survived the First World War. When the all clear sounded and the staff returned, they were so ashamed and embarrassed about leaving mother behind that they gave her the best of everything. Mother enjoyed ten days of luxury! She spent the next five years in the slums and gave birth to three more children, one born out of wedlock.

After the ten days had passed, my father sent a twelve-year-old boy to escort mother and her new baby on the train journey back to the rented rooms, even though he himself was not working and could well have gone to meet her. She was helped on to the train by one of the nurses, and finally made her way to her rooms. All was quiet. The rooms were even dirtier than when she'd left them. It was obvious that her husband had been sharing the place with females. My mother was not at all surprised at this, which is a sad reflection on both of their attitudes towards their marriage and family. No thought had been given to where the new baby would sleep, so she made a bed for me in a cardboard box wedged between two chairs.

23

"My first awareness came more in impressions than thoughts; impressions of an unhappy start in life.
My nostrils rebelled against the vile smells.
My ears closed to the excessively loud noises.
My eyes constantly looked away.
My taste spoiled by grease and lard. My flesh jerked away from the slightest touch. It was as though all my senses were at war with their environment, with no protection from mother or father."

— A Child's Thoughts

It would not be long before a pattern would develop in my life. I would alternate between being put in care and living in rented rooms in the slums. My life had started but it would not be a normal one. The experiences could crush me, or make me but I would lose a part of my childhood and that sense of loss would be a great burden to bear. Remnants of it are still with me today.

My birth took place as the war amongst nations escalated. Birthdays are supposed to be special days, a once-a-year event for each individual family member. Yet at no time during my childhood did my mother or my father even acknowledge my birthday, so, right into adulthood, I never attached any significance to the date.

My brother Bernard was born ten months after me, followed eighteen months later by Brian.

24

Dad was called up to join the army in February 1944. He witnessed the horrors of the concentration camps. While he was in the army, mother became pregnant by another man and gave birth to a baby girl in 1945. This meant that, as well as our half-brother, Donald, we now had a half-sister called Tracey. We never saw Tracey. She was given up for adoption from birth. We never knew who her father was. Twenty-eight years later mother claimed he was a man from London who already had six children of his own. Maybe she didn't really know who the father was.

If Mom had feelings for her children and if Dad was as bad as she later claimed him to be, then now he was away she had the opportunity to create a happy family home. She had regular army pay, Family Allowance and seven ration books. But as she so often said, she was different from most young mothers.

During that period, there was a dramatic increase in promiscuity and pregnancies amongst single girls.

Drink, cigarettes, nylon stockings, chocolates, additional money as well as a foreign accent charmed many a girl into giving herself to a young man in uniform. But mother was neither young nor single! She had six children but that didn't curb her lifestyle. Some people who knew the sort of life mother was leading during 1944 and 1945 have kept quiet about it because of the shame. Their silence, together with the remarks of those prepared to speak out, suggest that mother behaved more like an irresponsible young girl than a married woman with six children. Mother admitted years later that her lifestyle meant that she never considered her children. They were in rags and tatters while she was always smartly dressed in spite of clothes rationing. The neighbours even started a rumour that she was keeping a brothel!

> "I like it here. It's warm and there's hot food and children to play with and a big woman who smiles. But I know it won't last."
>
> — A Child's Thoughts

Sadly, when mother had the chance to make a fresh start to become a mother to her children she didn't take it. Instead she became a stranger to them and created more tension in the family by bearing, in Dad's words, 'another bastard child'. This was her contribution to the horror that was to come.

26

A LONE BOMBER AND A PREGNANT WOMAN

So my first five years and ten months were lived without any hugs or kisses or signs of affection. Instead there was the uncertainty of being separated from my brothers and sister. Aware of my physical and speech problems, I retreated into an isolated world of my own, despite my natural inclination and desire to be loved and to love.

Soon I was to leave the slums behind and move into the countryside. I would exchange the smelly cobbled courtyards of over-crowded back-to-back housing with their tiny, airless rooms for fields, hedge-rows, trees, cornfields, horses, cows and adventures that city-dwellers might dream of but would seldom experience.

That was when I began to live two lives: one behind the closed doors of our house, and the other out in the vast expanse of space, undisciplined and running wild in the fields, like Huckleberry Finn in Mark Twain's famous stories.

The sounds and smells of war were part and parcel of the first few years of my life. Those early days of confusion and uncertainty swept a torrent of contradictions and despair like a polluted river into my soul: the exodus from the slums, wartime rationing, poverty, cold and neglect. Slowly, I was emerging into an adult world – a world that for me was not a happy place. My first articulate memories and emotions on awakening into this so-called adult world were feelings of being unloved, unnoticed, unwanted and, saddest of all, not belonging.

By Christmas 1946 I was nearly five years old but I hardly knew my mother. She neglected me when I was with her and sent me into care when she was evacuated or having more babies. That winter mother collected all but one of her children from the various institutions she had left them in, to start a new life in a terraced council house in a farming community a few miles out of Birmingham. My family was one of the first to be rehoused in the countryside after the war. It was a golden opportunity for my parents to rebuild a new life away from the slums but that was a challenge they were not prepared to meet.

The war had ended in Europe and a new war was beginning at home. After their collective sufferings during the war, people and communities were determined to put things behind them and move forward. It was not that simple for the Hicks children. Their suffering was inflicted on them by their own parents. It restricted every opportunity for development and growth. It stripped them of dignity and damaged them mentally, physically and emotionally. This was the sad lot of the Hicks children who were often separated from their parents and from each other. Although the family was reunited to start a new life away from the slums, the children were still condemned to a cruel, cruel childhood.

When my mother was pregnant with my half-sister, my older brothers, my sister and I were sent to a place called Erdington Cottage Homes. My two younger brothers were sent to another Home in Wales. Erdington Cottage Homes was an institution built with funds donated by Sir Josiah Mason, an industrialist whose wealth had come from making fountain pens. Sir Josiah gave generously to the poor of Birmingham as well as contributing to the educational and cultural well-being of the city. The name Erdington Cottage Homes was warm and welcoming and indeed it was a place of security with regular hot food, plenty of hot water, and bathrooms and toilets inside the buildings! I knew, even though I was only five, that I could not count on staying for long. Nevertheless, Christmas was only a few days away, and with excitement in the Homes mounting, I had something good to look forward to – or so I thought.

CHAPTER 2
DARK CLOUDS
ON THE HORIZON

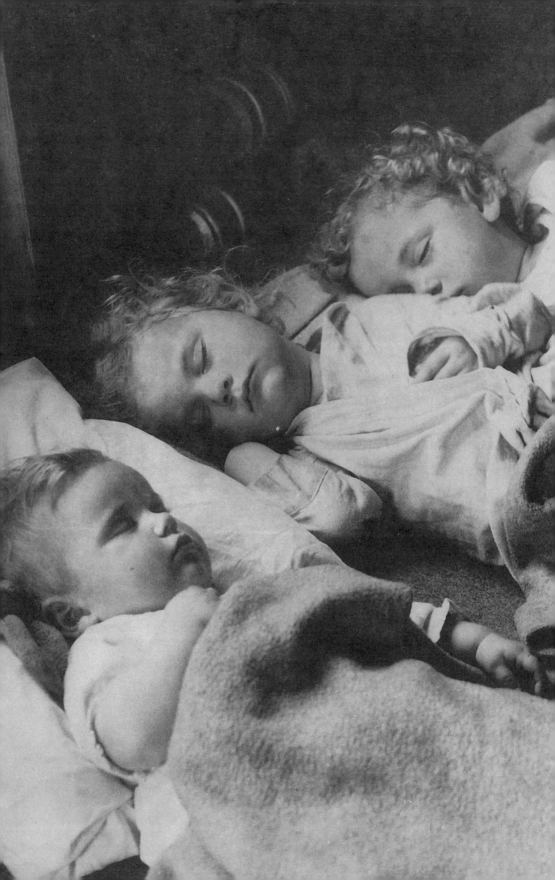

CHAPTER 2
DARK CLOUDS ON THE HORIZON

My father, Mr William Hicks, was born in Sheffield, a huge industrial city known throughout the world for its manufacture of cutlery and stainless steel. Dad was a wild young man, always seeking trouble. He left Sheffield under a cloud. Various stories circulated about him. One of these stories was that he had left behind a married woman, pregnant with his child. Another story was that he refused to work and was constantly rowing with his parents. He left after a violent argument during which he physically fought with his mother.

> "Mother and father have lots of children, but I seldom see them. I seldom play with them. I don't know them. We are strangers to each other.
>
> They call this a family."
>
> — A Child's Thoughts

33

In his early twenties he moved to the slum area of Birmingham where accommodation was very cheap and where a runaway could disappear. He stayed with Mrs Gee who kept a huge boarding house. Her male lodgers were provided with single beds in dormitories but the place lacked even the most basic amenities of hygiene.

Dad was tall, fit and handsome and extremely attracted to the opposite sex. A proud man, he always wanted to look bigger and grander than he was, although in fact he was uneducated and had left school at fourteen. He married my mother in October 1939. By then she was seven months pregnant with John and already had a young son, Donald, who had been born in the January. Mother gave birth to two children in the same calendar year and twelve months later Jean, my elder sister, was born. I was only fourteen months younger than Jean. Bernard, my younger brother was born the following December and Brian, the youngest of us all, only eighteen months later.

> "Mom has lots of children, but not lots of love. Maybe no love at all."
> — A Child's Thoughts

Dad seldom accepted responsibility for his own actions and, as his life unfolded, would not accept his obligations to the five children he had fathered with my mother.

My mother, Winifred Hampton, was born in the slums of Birmingham but thanks to her grandparents she was sheltered from much of their harsh reality. A strong, well-built woman she always felt different from those around her because of the privileges she had enjoyed. However, like father, she was overly attracted to the opposite sex and, like him, was incapable of accepting responsibility for her own actions and for the children she gave birth to.

During her life, she had children by three or four men. One child, conceived while her husband was away at war, was surrendered for adoption. It is believed that this little girl was of mixed race.

So children were conceived from a marriage made in Hell who innocently would have to endure its pain.

For the first six years of my life I am dependent on the memories of others, as the only impressions I can recall are emotions and feelings that I have carried through into my adult life. I do have an awareness and general recollection of loud noises and threats, of horrible smells and of constantly being told to 'Shut up!'

Mrs Gee, the big unkempt woman who looked after

35

the boarding house told me that I used to toddle around the cobbled courtyard between the back-to-back houses saying, 'Gib me djam. Gib me djam!' No doubt somebody had once given me some jam and I was always begging for more. She also told me that, most of the time, the small children ran around naked except for a short shirt. Of all my nightmares, and there were many, to be running around dressed only in a shirt that covered so little that I was conscious of being naked, continued into adulthood, so obviously my childhood experience had left a deep impression on me. We would wee in the gutter and were known as 'gutter children' and would grow up to be 'street boys' and 'ragamuffins' – common terms for children from the slums.

Dad regularly lodged with Mrs Gee because our home was overcrowded. The overcrowding got worse when Grandmother and her children squatted with us after she was bombed out of her home. During those first six years of my life, my family seldom stopped in one place. We moved from squalor to squalor and each time mother had another baby we would be taken into care for two or three weeks, only to return to a different home. A hundred thousand houses, many of them slums, were destroyed or damaged by German bombs and alternative accommodation was hard to find.

Dark Clouds on the Horizon

Once, mother found a slum house with three empty rooms, each above the other, and we squatted there. While we were there, one of my brothers dropped me on my head. I was rushed to hospital, but nothing untoward was found. Many years later I was told that possibly a communication membrane linking the left and right hand sides of the brain had been broken or damaged and this could account for me having both a creative and an analytical mind, which apparently is rare.

During those years, I never got to know my parents. They were strangers to me, especially my father. He joined the army when I was three years of age and my mother returned to living her promiscuous life.

> "Can she be my mother? Is this my real mother who will love me, talk to me, listen to me and care for me? No: I don't think she really is my mother!"
>
> — A Child's Thoughts

I can remember very distinctly being taken to Erdington Cottage Homes. It was a warm and caring place but I felt insecure and unable to relax because I knew that one day a stranger would come and take me away. My first clear memory of that is for ever fixed in my mind. It was a few days before Christmas 1946. I'd been taken to the Infirmary ready for my mother to collect me. A woman stood in the doorway. She was holding a little six-year-old girl by the hand. This was the woman who had given birth

37

to me during the blitz on Birmingham. She had come to take me back with her to a new home. I knew she was my mother but she was a stranger to me whose very smell repelled me.

I was disappointed, despondent, confused and disorientated. What I had feared most was actually happening. The Homes had been a shelter from the storm, somewhere I felt safe, somewhere which gave me a warm glow. One of the staff, a large, loving lady took me into her arms once and I relaxed into her soft motherly bosom. For one moment, I lost myself in the scent of her warm flesh and caring heart. But with mother's appearance on the doorstep, my heart sank as I knew I would have to leave this warm, clean, safe place where there was plenty of food and children sang and played games. I would be taken away from people who didn't shout, scream or threaten me. I was not afraid of their touch because these people cared about me and they showed they cared. The other children had been telling me that Christmas in the Homes was an extra-special time. Many voluntary organizations would

> "I don't know who I am, why I am here or how long I will stay here, but I know it's better than where I was before. That was horrible.
> They tell me I can stay for Christmas. I don't know what Christmas is."
>
> — A Child's Thoughts —

bring gifts of clothes, food and games. The turkeys and chickens would be filled with apples and stuffing! I had never heard of such a thing and I found the picture very funny indeed. I had to leave all this, for somewhere that would be smelly, dirty, cold and unfriendly.

Hot food and plenty of it was more important to children from the slums than possibly anything else that anyone could give them. That Christmas would have been the first Christmas when I would have felt both peace and happiness. Another eight years passed before I experienced a real Christmas, when the NSPCC took myself and two of my brothers away to a seaside resort called Weston-Super-Mare.

> They tell me I will have hot food and lots of presents, but I don't believe them.
> I know somebody will take me away.
> I wish I could stop for Christmas and have hot food and lots of presents."
>
> — A Child's Thoughts

I did not know the lady who brought me down the stairs to meet mother. She smiled at me, not realising that I felt as if I was being led as a lamb to the slaughter. Her smile reminded me of the Cheshire cat in Alice in Wonderland, a smile that kept appearing then disappearing in my dreams. Mother did not speak to me. She talked to the lady.

39

ROBERT HICKS

When she signed some papers it felt as though I was being given away. I certainly didn't feel as if I was going home for there was no joy in my heart.

I knew it was cold outside because it had been snowing and we had been kept in for the past few days. The winter of 1946 was recorded as one of the coldest of the century. My child's mind associated bad things with the cold: cold face, cold hands, cold feet, cold house, cold rooms and eventually bad things that happened in a cold kitchen in the early hours of the morning. The six-year-old girl mother had brought with her was Jean, my sister. She was already cold as there was thick snow on the ground. Mother wore gloves but Jean had newspaper wrapped round her hands and feet.

The day before I left the Homes, I was given a bar of Cadbury's chocolate and a hoop-la game. This was an early Christmas present as the staff knew I would miss out at Christmas. In the hustle and bustle of leaving, I left behind the pennies I had been given at chapel each week, the bar of chocolate and the hoop-la game. The fact that I forgot those precious items clearly illustrates how confused and upset I was at the time.

The heavy door of the Homes closed behind us and, even as I write, I can hear the sound of that door

40

as it shut. Although I would later go into other institutions, that was the last time I would set foot in Erdington Cottage Homes; the last time I would feel the warmth and love of the caring big-bosomed lady with the comforting smile. Her absence in my life left an aching void that lasted for many, many years!

The walk from the big house, past the magnificent clock tower, down to the tram stop was a long and cold one.

I put my hands in my pockets and followed my mother and sister. They kept telling me to keep up with

> "Today, I walked a long way from the warm Home to a cold house and it was very, very cold."
> — A Child's Thoughts

them and my little feet were forced into a trot in response. Eventually we boarded the tram. It was a new experience for me. The top part of the tram was open and it was freezing sitting there in the winter but it had to be endured. Mother and Jean sat together and I sat behind them. Occasionally Jean said something to mother, but I have no recollection of their conversation as I felt too miserable to join in.

At last we reached Birmingham city centre. As it was Christmas-time, the shops' lights were dazzling. Some of the larger shops had made a real effort with their Christmas decorations. In spite of the cold numbing my senses, I realised that this was a big world that was totally unknown to me. It was strange and unfamiliar and made me feel unsure as though I had arrived in an alien place. I was scared by the thought that I was going backwards instead of forwards – back to a place of no escape.

The journey south from Birmingham to Bartley Green took about forty minutes on a number 12 double-decker blue and yellow bus. There were so many stops on the way to Bartley Green that mother allowed me to sit upstairs while she and Jean stayed downstairs. I looked through the dirty windows at all the large houses that had been built. After the destruction of the bombing raids there was evidence of new buildings and fresh repair works in every direction.

Eventually, the landscape of large houses gave way to a few scattered houses, separated by fields covered with snow. I can remember the bus-conductress calling out 'California!' which I thought was a name I already knew. When I was older I realised that this local district had been named after a place in the United States of America, made famous in an Al Jolson song, *California, here I come...* The bus conductress was smothered in layer upon layer of woollen clothes out of which peered her small face. She looked so funny that I couldn't help but laugh to myself. In spite of all my problems I could always laugh at something funny and one day I learnt to laugh at myself as well as at other people. Deep down inside me I desperately wanted to be happy and joyful in other people's company.

'Stonehouse Lane!' called out the conductress. Jean shouted up to me to come down. Stonehouse Lane was two stops before the terminus at the top of a winding hill called Jiggins Lane. We got off the bus in front of a long row of terraced houses. It wasn't the sight of the terraced houses that I first remembered, but the silence and the absence of the nauseating smells so distinctive of the slums. The blue and yellow bus quickly disappeared, its lights fading into the distance. All around us was quiet. This was a new world, very different from what I had anticipated. The vastness of the empty space all around over-whelmed me.

> "I don't like it when it's quiet. Bad things can happen in the quiet."
> — A Child's Thoughts

In the noisy slums and in the busy Homes I had never experienced silence, certainly not like this. At first I was afraid of the silence, and I have to confess, to this day, I do not like being on my own. I find it easier to relax when people are around me and I can hear the radio or television in the background. A psychoanalyst might, I suspect, conclude that my need for people and sound is a result of listening in silence for that dreaded bang of the back door, heralding Dad's presence and the fear that brought with it.

Many years ago Bartley Green had been a farming community but it had fallen on hard times. At one time, it was a centre for hand made nails, but with the advance of the Industrial Revolution, who wanted hand-made nails? The farms and the district were in decline and Birmingham city council took over many of the farms for housing developments. Not much building took place while I lived in Bartley Green but after I left thousands of houses were built on the farmland and the entire area became a massive estate.

We crossed over the road. There was a wide green verge, then a footpath which led along the small gardens in front of the terraced houses. There were around thirty houses in the row and, except for a bungalow opposite (later converted into the village shop) and a few scattered private houses, Stonehouse Lane was surrounded by open fields. The houses were all joined together apart from an occasional shared arched passageway which led to the back gardens of the houses. We had such a passageway down the side of our house.

To the left of our house was a gate into the front garden of number 337. Mr and Mrs Taylor, a retired couple, lived there. They had a lodger who looked older than the Taylors themselves. He had been injured in the war and never left the house. It was quite common for people to take in lodgers as it helped families on a low budget to supplement their incomes, and the additional ration book was useful.

Mr Taylor had kindly lit a fire for us in the family room of 335 Stonehouse Lane. Had he not done so the house would have been icily cold. Mother opened the door and the most peculiar smell imaginable hit me. The local council had emulsioned all the walls and ceilings to clean up the house for us and I suspect the warmth from the fire had drawn the gases from the paint. At first it was overpowering. Number 335 was not a friendly house and this stench was hardly welcoming! The house was small by comparison with Erdington Cottage Homes but it was substantially more spacious than the rented rooms we had occupied in the slums.

I cannot remember whether we ate anything that night but I was still hungry when we went to bed. Hungry, sad, and confused I simply did what I was told mechanically.

We all slept in one bed. The sheets were not clean like the ones at the Homes. The thin blanket was not sufficient to keep us warm so mother had to lay her coat on top. She had done nothing to prepare the house for us children. I later discovered that we had to

ROBERT HICKS

leave the comfort and celebration of Christmas at the Homes so that mother could claim the additional Army Allowance that increased with each child, as well as the Family Allowance and the all-important ration books which she had been deprived of during our stay in institutions while she was in a nursing home giving birth to our half-sister. If mother had really loved us, I don't believe she would have removed us from the Homes just a few days before Christmas, knowing that she had nothing to offer us in the midst of a severe winter except a bitterly cold house that had been unoccupied for some time and no prospect of a decent meal on Christmas Day.

> "I cannot understand why Mom has taken me away from a warm house and hot food and children to play with and Christmas. I feel so cold and hungry and I don't think Christmas is going to come to our house."
>
> — A Child's Thoughts

I had a restless night, awoken by the cold whenever the sheet, blanket and coat were pulled off me. In the end, I tucked part of the long sleeve of the coat under my body. In time, I learnt to put both feet down the coat sleeves to give me extra warmth at night, as well as wearing my own coat to bed.

The next morning couldn't come soon enough for me. We warmed ourselves by the heat of the gas stove that had been installed. Gas for heating and lighting had only recently been installed in the terraced houses. Many more years elapsed before electricity was connected – far too late for me to enjoy its benefit!

The terraced houses had been cheaply built in the 1920's. In the late 1940's they were occupied either by families who had been rehoused from the slums or by working-class people who had previously rented rooms. The waiting list for such council property ran into tens of thousands. All the occupants of these houses felt privileged, although the newer houses built in their thousands on the surrounding farmland would have been even more prized. With dad in the army and Mom surrounded by six children the Hicks' family were able to jump the queue to be rehoused, an exceedingly long queue at that! Friends and relations believed we were very blessed, as indeed we were, to be allocated a house.

From the front door you entered a small hallway which led into a small room on the left and the family room on the right. No one ever made use of the small room except on dubious occasions when my father was in prison. It was the family room that became the all-purpose room. There were two boilers behind the cast-iron stove which could provide hot water for the house. I can't remember there being hot water in the house

47

"The perfect FRIEND is one who knows the best and worst of us and loves us just the same."

very often, which suggests a shortage of coal. The coal house, with its single-brick wall, was somewhere Bernard, Donald and Brian would occasionally spend the night rather than come inside the house and suffer a beating. To the left of the fire was a small wooden cupboard. It became a dreaded place because that was where Dad kept his wide, heavy army belt – a belt we all feared. There was neither table nor chair in the room (although a table and chairs came later) but there was a French-style settee which mother had acquired. In one corner, the gas meter was enclosed in a wooden box. That corner became my salvation from the mental, emotional and physical terrors of the house. I had already started retreating within myself, and that corner became my entire world. It was where I could play my own thought games or copy out words, where I could block out the cursing and the cruelty which took place around me. That one small corner was exclusively mine. The memory of it never faded or lost its importance, and it remains for ever a symbol of my ultimate escape from the Hell I went through as a child.

There were no pictures on the walls, although someone had left a small text in calligraphy, which read, 'The Perfect Friend is one who knows the best and worst of us... and loves us just the same'. I read those words many times, and everything in me would reject what they were saying, yet I longed with all my heart that they might be true. Strangely, the words mocked me in my childhood, but at the same time they offered me the ray of hope that I so desperately needed.

For the next ten years of my life this house in Bartley Green was void of any friend. It was as if God himself had deserted it and had no desire at all to visit it. I longed for that 'Perfect Friend' countless times but that 'Friend' never turned up at 335.

It took only one stride from entering the house to reach the stairs. Adjacent to the staircase was a narrow passage which led to the rear of the house with a toilet on the left and the kitchen on the right. The toilet had originally been accessed from outside the house but the council had knocked out a doorway to make it an indoor lavatory. The narrow kitchen housed a newly-

> "What is a friend?
> It must be someone who does not expect to gain anything from you, but wants to be with you whenever he can.
> Maybe no-one in the world has a real friend.
> I don't think I will ever have a real friend.
> I wonder if I could be a real friend to somebody.
> One day, I will try."
>
> — A Child's Thoughts

installed copper wash tub. A gas ring underneath the tub heated the water to boiling point. Clothes were thrown into the tub and swirled around with a wooden stick. There was no soap powder. Before the clothes went into the tub, we had to rub them with a bar of soap. The soap was not like the soft tablets we have today, but like a hard solid brick. By the age of eleven I was washing Dad's shirts as well as my own, making sure I rubbed the collar and cuffs thoroughly with the bar of soap. The gas stove was small and yellow. It had been wedged into the place where once there had been an open fire. The other feature of the kitchen was the stark and barren pantry at the far end. The pantry and the toilet were the coldest places in the house. The pantry had a large, slightly cracked, marble slab on which fresh and dairy foods could be kept cool. We had little use for it.

> "My sister has a room all to herself. I wish I had a room to myself, then I could have a bed to myself instead of sharing it with all my brothers."
>
> — A Child's Thoughts

Upstairs were three small bedrooms and a bathroom. Mother and father's bedroom was on the left. It was the only room that had a small gas fire. As it was above the unused room, it was cold. What took place in that room belonged to the chill of shadows and darkness. The boys' room was above the sitting room. In the winter we would sleep five to one bed, three at the head and two at the foot, in order to keep warm. The other bed had wire springs protruding from the mattress, which made it very uncomfortable. In the summer time, both beds were used and I had to learn where to position myself so that the springs did not attack me!

Jean's room was a small box room. She could lock it and woe betide us if we entered her room without permission. Jean kept her room tidy and put pictures on the wall. It was a real contrast to the sparseness of the boys' room. Her room was the only bedroom that offered any comfort from the curse my parents had brought into 335.

At the back of the house upstairs was a narrow bathroom housing a cast-iron bath and washbasin. I have very few memories of having a bath in that tub. Although the boiler behind the living room fire provided hot water for the bathroom, there was never enough for a decent bath. At school, we showered before Physical Education. Recognising our need of a good shower, the teacher insisted that we stayed under the flowing water much longer than we wanted – especially if the water was cold. Maybe the cold water took longer to clean us!

The house was lit throughout by gas. When the

local council renovated the house they made sure that every gas light was working and installed the fragile lamp mantles that gave off the light. It didn't take long before the only lamps left in our house were in the living room and the kitchen, because whenever moths broke the lamps in those two rooms the lamps from the other rooms were simply transferred since they were so expensive to replace.

I wanted to explore my new environment so I wrapped paper around my feet and put on my hand-me-down clothes which the well-meaning supporters of Erdington Cottage Homes had given me. Outside it was cold but the sun was shining and what had been shrouded in darkness the previous evening, now filled me with wonder. In the slums we did not have the benefit of fresh air or light, and although both were available at the Homes, we had been kept inside the houses, probably because of the bad weather and so that we would come to no harm. Snow covered the trees, fields, bushes, the long privet hedges in their different shapes and sizes, the garden gate and so much more! It was a wonderland! It was fairyland! My eyes and my imagination were overpowered by what I saw. I was awe struck by the beauty of it all.

There was nobody around but as I turned to go back into the house I heard Mrs Taylor's voice, 'Hello, little boy. Do you want to come in and have some juice?' I looked at Mrs Taylor. She was a thin, elderly lady. Even though I was very young, I could see there was love and sadness in her eyes. Her two children had died many years ago. It must have been a terrible blow for her. My eyes and my face opened up and I gave her the biggest smile I could give. As I smiled she smiled, and the kindness she would show me in future years was proof enough that my innocent young face had stolen her heart. In those early days, when I was out of the house, I was always smiling and the older ladies in the lane would often remark on it. Slowly, I lost that openness and retreated ever further within myself. It would be many years before I would feel relaxed enough to smile naturally, rather than forcing a smile to hide my sadness and pain.

Mrs Taylor's house was a total contrast to ours. The whole house was warm. Although there was lino in the hallway, the other rooms were carpeted. The house was full of old furniture, some was theirs and some belonged to their lodger. I was told to sit on an upright chair even though my feet did not touch the floor. Mr Barnett, the lodger, was sitting in his old reclining chair. The small room on the ground floor was his bedroom as he could not climb the stairs.

Mrs Taylor brought in two cups of coffee that looked delicious and my glass of juice which she had

53

warmed. The glass was too hot for me to hold, so I had to wait for it to cool down. Mr Barnett asked me whether I liked magic. I had heard of magic, but I did not know what it was, so I simply nodded, 'Yes'. Then he picked up a very long wooden tube, placed one end to his eye, and began to rotate part of the tube at the other end. He pointed the tube at the light coming through the window. After a moment he said, 'Come and have a look.' When I looked through the tube I was amazed to see a brilliant pattern of shapes and colours. Then he began to move the top end of the tube and the colours and shapes kept changing. I was fascinated. This was real magic. Mr Barnett pointed to the word 'Kaleidoscope' on the tube. It meant nothing to me as I couldn't read.

> "They work all the time on their garden. It's as though it is all they have in the whole world... their garden. There must be something special about a garden."
>
> — A Child's Thoughts

It must have been obvious to Mrs Taylor that I had difficulty in speaking, but as I was so young she and others simply put it down to the fact that I had come from the slums and had lazy speech. It was not until I started work that an ex-nurse would diagnose the cause of my speech problem.

Although Mr. Taylor had retired he continued to

look after the gardens of manor houses and stately homes – or maybe they were just big houses! Most of his life had been spent gardening and he had many funny stories to tell about the lives of posh people. Mr. and Mrs Taylor became my friends, even though they kept themselves to themselves as far as my family was concerned. The gardens of Stonehouse Lane were included in the 'Best Kept Garden Competition' and the Taylors were always the local winners and often the regional winners. They deserved to win because they both worked really hard on their plot. It was a constant joy to see the change in colour and design year by year.

Just before Christmas, mother went back to the city to collect my elder brothers from the Homes. I can only assume that Jean and I stayed behind, because I cannot remember going with her. I asked mother to make sure she brought my shiny pennies, bar of chocolate and hoop-la game back with her. When, eventually, the boys returned, I was only given the game. My brothers had eaten the chocolate and Donald said he couldn't find the pennies. I knew he had kept them for himself! What annoyed me for many months was that my brothers had not even saved me a piece of the chocolate, and it would be a long time before I would have the chance to taste chocolate again.

Bernard and Brian came back from Wales where they had been in care and by Christmas the whole family was together except for Dad who was in the army. He was involved in helping to clean up one of the concentration camps and saw for himself the terrible effects of war. I found it amazing that someone who had witnessed the inhumanity of man to man would ever deliberately injure another human being, let alone his own children, but Dad's angry, abusive, violent nature which was stimulated by strong drink was not tempered by the unbelievable cruelty he had seen.

As Christmas Day dawned, I kept thinking about the fortunate children at Erdington Cottage Home. They would be having a party and celebrating, enjoying hot food and games. When we woke up on Christmas morning there were stockings on our beds. We opened them eagerly. Two thirds of each stocking was full of crumpled paper and on the top was an apple, an orange and a few boiled sweets. That was the only Christmas when I can remember having any kind of stocking. John, however, was given a fountain pen with ink and a notebook, which he treasured. I always thought his handwriting was beautiful and I envied him that fountain pen! Jean received a second-hand doll's house and a set of miniature kitchen furniture which became very special to her. I suspect mother had these few toys given to her, because the rest of us got nothing. Mother had, however, treated herself to new (or newish) clothes – a dress, an overcoat and shoes.

Mr Taylor disguised himself as a tramp and stood out in the cold playing a tune on his fiddle. We felt sorry for him, invited him in and then discovered his true identity! Later, we stood on his doorstep and sang the first verse of 'O come, all ye faithful', the only Christmas carol we knew. For this we were each rewarded with a glass of hot juice. All of us loved Mr and Mrs Taylor, yet, strangely, we never confided in them or revealed to them how bad our situation had become. They never questioned us about our home life as such enquiries would have been seen as nosiness in those days.

> "Other children in the Lane have told me they get cards and presents for their birthdays. Only John and Jean have got presents in our house. Bernard, Brian and I do not. I wonder why we never get cards or presents. Mom and Dad spend their money when they go out every night. Maybe that's the reason why."
>
> — A Child's Thoughts

57

ROBERT HICKS

That Christmas of 1946 left me in despair. We had been cheated of the real Christmas which we would have had within the warmth and security of the institutions. Mother was fully aware that she was bringing us to a house that was inadequately prepared and in which there was no food. She had not provided any sort of family Christmas and though there were charities that would have helped her, she had not approached them.

When we were reunited that Christmas we children did not realise that while we'd been away mother had given birth to her seventh child, a baby girl. After Mom deserted us a few years later, Dad repeatedly reminded us that this baby girl was a bastard child. There was nothing in Mom's behaviour to suggest that she had recently given her baby up for adoption. Her story was that the father of her child was a married man from London who already had six children. She herself certainly neglected her children while Dad was away. The neighbours gossiped among themselves and surmised that she was keeping a brothel. Suspicions were raised by the fact that she had chocolates, cigarettes, stockings and additional money

> "I remember the slums; the smells, the noises and the children. I wish they could all come out into the countryside. Bartley Green is big enough for everyone!"
>
> — A Child's Thoughts

for other luxuries and that the only real furniture she
brought with her to 335 was the French style settee,
which amongst poor and working class families was
associated with loose living. In those last two years of
the war, she certainly had extra money for drinking and
parties and something inside me finds it hard to believe
that cash came from her normal family budget. That
period of her life remains a mystery, so if wrong
conclusions are drawn she must be forgiven, but
somehow I do not think that is the case.

Maybe that Christmas in 1946
she felt she needed her children
around her having just surrendered
her newborn child. Maybe she
wanted the additional money and
ration coupons. Whatever the reasons,
it was a miserable time for us children
especially as the bad weather forced us to stay indoors
with nothing to do except play hoop-la. As for me, I
felt I did not belong. I spent Christmas as a stranger,
and that feeling grew stronger and stronger as time
passed. I now know that other members of the family
felt exactly the same as me, but for other reasons. We
had no one to whom we could express our feelings, so
we had to bear them inwardly. I was aware, even at that
age, that I was not speaking properly and although my
own family could understand me, I knew I had a real

59

ROBERT HICKS

> "I went on a long walk to where the children play on swings while their mothers talk to each other. The mothers looked so happy talking and they never seemed to stop. The children looked so happy playing and they never seemed to stop either. I am glad that some families have nice mothers and children. I wish Dad and Mom would come to the playground and see how happy people can be."
>
> — A Child's Thoughts

problem which contributed to me feeling left out. Little children feel things deeply and can become frustrated if they are ignored and not understood. There were many things going on inside me, but I had no one to share them with. I was full of questions, which multiplied as I grew older, but there was no one to whom I could direct them, and even if there had been someone, I would have had great difficulty in articulating and expressing my thoughts. These were the outward signs of a dyslexic mind, compounded by my speech impediment.

That cold, cold winter was a winter to be endured and not enjoyed, even though the covering of pure white snow fascinated a little boy from the slums and institutions beyond belief. Slowly the winter passed and spring was upon us. We started to explore the green fields around us and the farms. Soon we realised that there were other local children of

60

our own age and, before long, various harmless gangs and groups were formed. Donald used to go off with the older group. John and Jean, who at home were always fighting over nothing, had their own groups too. To begin with Brian and Bernard used to follow me around but in time, they drew closer to Jean and when she was sent away they stayed together. Being one of the middle offspring in a large family resulted in me feeling that I neither belonged to my older or younger siblings. That was how I felt and it contributed to my deep sense of being alone.

We were told that Dad would soon be home from the war and, in our innocence, we looked forward to his homecoming. We did not yet know the dark side of Dad's nature. Our minds were filled with the great exploits of the war and how victorious our heroes had been against the wicked Germans and Japanese. The way these enemy nationalities were talked about and depicted in comics made me apprehensive of them right into adulthood. Later, black people were portrayed in a similarly negative and racist manner and, again, it would take many years for me to overcome my mistrust and disquiet about them. To my shame, I have to admit that I did form a strong antipathy towards Germans, Japanese and all black-skinned peoples. Only slowly did I begin to accept them, value their uniqueness and respect their individuality.

61

After Dad was demobbed, he arrived home. He was accompanied by another man who was going to stop for a day or two. We were all over Dad. He wore a huge army overcoat with shining buttons and an impressive leather army belt and he looked like Errol Flynn. When he was sober, Dad was a congenial and boastful person, always seeking the limelight. If we had visitors from the slums, he would play shadow-boxing, which all the boys enjoyed until it got out of hand. However, he rarely, and only briefly, showed us any kindness. He never took us out for walks to discover the farmland around us, or to the park which was not far away, or up to the nearby giant reservoir that used to feed Birmingham with its fresh water. There were bluebell woods within walking distance where everyone else took their children, but neither mother or father ever took us. The lifestyle they both followed centred around them, not the family.

Not far from us was a public playground and park stretching out towards a residential area where people owned their own houses. Mothers would bring their children to play on the swings and roundabouts and I believed the playground belonged to them and not to us. When I went there alone, I always felt I was an impostor. I was really uncomfortable, convinced that the mothers were staring at me. They probably were. My clothes were a give-away as to my social class, and no doubt their protective instincts for their little ones were alerted. I can never remember Mom or Dad ever going to the park or exploring the countryside. It was as though they were dyed-in-the-wool city people, drawn only to city-type attractions such as the picture house and pub.

> "I know how to count the stars in the sky!
> I make a circle with my first finger and thumb and stretch it from my eye until I can count a hundred stars. Then I move the circle around the sky and count how many circles it needs to cover the sky.
> There are hundreds and hundreds of stars!"
> — A Child's Thoughts

Dad had left the slums to join the army nearly two years earlier. While he was away, mother was involved in wild parties and immoral relationships. Her reckless social life at this time, reflected badly on her, and it is

63

something her children can never forget.

Mother was free from any fear or threat of Dad's violent temper while he was away. She had six children under the age of eight, and all of them would be put into care many times. Even at critical times when her children needed her, she would go out leaving her younger brother, Tommy, to look after us. Many other families from the slums came to live in Bartley Green and they too would experience sad and tragic events but it was neither natural nor typical for mothers from the slums to deny love and warmth to their own children. My mother was not loving. At a time far into the future her children would find that they had no filial love for her, which demonstrates the eternal principle that, 'what we sow, we will most surely reap'. The fact that we had never experienced motherly affection did not prevent all of us from feeling a huge vacuum within us, one that could only be filled by our mother's love. That vacuum is a curse and a burden to be carried throughout our lives.

Inside 335 I would experience Hell while outside I revelled in the miracle of nature. A paradox and a contradiction, yet for me this was reality. Hell and Paradise existed together. What happened inside the home pushed me down, deeper and deeper into an ever-decreasing smaller existence. What happened outside drew me up and out as I ran wild and free away from the terrible atmosphere in the place called 'home'.

C H A P T E R 3

INSIDE AND OUTSIDE:
HELL AND PARADISE

CHAPTER 3

INSIDE AND OUTSIDE: HELL AND PARADISE

In those early days at Bartley Green, I was forever humming and talking to myself. Talking to myself was a private matter, but the humming got on the nerves of those around me. It became an annoying habit that continued until I started work and the staff in the shop forced me to stop before it drove them mad! Humming created a rhythm within me that allowed me to bend to the force of the increasingly uncomfortable emotional storms at home.

"I annoy everyone with my humming. Always humming to myself.
It soothes me.
It helps me think.
It helps me live.
Living is not easy,
except when I am alone
...alone in the fields,
near the old farm buildings ...
away from home.

Listening to the birds sing, I know why they are happy. They are outside, not inside number 335."

— A Child's Thoughts

It maintained a vibration in my mouth which helped to relieve the tension within my dyslexic mind and endure what was happening around me. My parents were strangers to me. The three older children were not on my wavelength and the younger ones belonged to the childhood years that I was leaving behind. I was alone.

> "I know people think I am crazy because I talk to myself, but if I don't do it, I will never learn to speak."
> — A Child's Thoughts

Alone. Humming. Talking to myself. If anyone had heard me they would not have understood me, because of my speech impediment. However, by talking out loud I was beginning to develop muscles in the back of my throat as well as at the back of my tongue.

My inner conversation at that time ran along predictable lines. It concerned the Christmas when mother had taken me away from Erdington Cottage Homes and the big lady with the motherly smell who had often given me a cuddle

When I was in bed with my four brothers I always slept on the outside and my strong, elder brother took the greater share of the blanket and coat. I would remember the clean warm bed in the institution which had been all mine.

Then there were the dreams, dreadful dreams, mostly about food. I would see myself wearing only a shirt that was too short for me and trying to pull it down to hide my nakedness. I would be crying to people for food, carrying an empty, chipped enamel plate, but with no spoon, knife or fork. Sometimes, in the dream, I would come to the window of someone's house in which there was light and warmth and laughter. The curtain would be drawn aside and the children would look out and start laughing. Eventually one of them would throw out some food, but it never landed on my plate, so I was always looking for it in the gutter.

In another dream I was again wearing the shirt that was far too short and holding a plate piled high with Christmas turkey. It was surrounded by all kinds of hot vegetables that we'd been promised in Erdington Cottage Homes and had so looked forward to. Because I was holding the plate with both hands I could not eat any of the food. Instead, my mother and father, one with a fork and the other with a knife, laughed and joked while they consumed everything on the plate.

Another dream was of a deep well. Again I carry the

69

chipped enamel plate and wear the same short shirt. I climb into the bucket and descend into the darkness, away from people, hoping that there may be some food in the well that I can consume alone. It was always cold in the well and I would wake from my dream still descending. As I talked to myself and played alone, I longed to be able to say things that people would understand. I wanted so much to be accepted for who I was and included rather than have the other children poke fun at me. How I craved to belong to the sun and the warmth, to have a normal family who lived an ordinary life. I was desperate to come in from the cold.

Alone. Humming. Talking to myself. Dreaming and all the time, the rippling brooks and green fields cried out to me, 'Run, Bobby, run! Run, Bobby, run.' The urge was always there and I needed to run, but apart from running into the fields, there was no escape for me.

For the next ten years, I hummed. It relieved the tensions in my mind and the vibrations were soothing. I developed my own particular way of talking, never realising that all I needed was a simple operation. I dreamt every night – vivid dreams that continued long, long after those ten years.

So, I was born into a violent world and caught up

in a web of powerful contradictions. The Great Depression of the 1930's harmed millions upon millions psychologically. They could not rid themselves of the fear of want, even when there was no reason to be afraid. Then there was Hollywood which created a fantasy world. Add to this, World War Two. For the first few years of my life, the horror of man's inhumanity to man was in full flood and in that process weapons of awesome destruction were used. The world witnessed two solitary bombs that wiped out entire cities. The horrific power of these atomic bombs cast a cloud of dread over all the world and would continue to do so for generations to come.

> "I can't understand it! I want to be happy in my new home with all the family, but I don't want to come home until it is dark, because then I can crawl into bed without Mom or Dad knowing. I don't think they miss me anyway. I don't understand it."
> — A Child's Thoughts

I had learnt before I could crawl not to cry out loud. The cruel abuse that took place behind closed doors took various forms. Looking back, I realise that the one which most affected me was not being recognised by my natural parents as having any worth. Lack of human love and affection is one thing, to be positively rejected is another, but not to be valued by

71

> "The worm doesn't like coming out of the ground because it is dangerous. The birds might eat it.
> I like getting out of the house because it is safer outside. The worm stops in the dark, afraid to come into the light. I stay as long as I can in the light, afraid of going back into the dark house.
> I am glad I am not a worm, but I wish I was not afraid of the night at home."
>
> — A Child's Thoughts

parents as special can leave at the very least an uncertain vacuum deep within a child for many years if not for an entire lifetime.

I was barely six years of age when I was taken out of the security of the institution for 'Children in Need of Care and Protection' which, although it lacked family life and personal love, did provide warmth and comfort, hot food, children to play with, a good night's sleep in clean sheets and a bed that I didn't have to share with four brothers.

When I was removed from the institution, heard the big doors close behind me and felt the extreme winter cold on my face, I knew that life would never be the same again. A terror more piercing than the winter chill filled my little body with fear. My first six years had taught me that moving to a new house was no guarantee of living in better conditions.

It is difficult to describe in words the contrast

between the slums and the open farmland. 'Slumland' was dirt and squalor, the smell of cheap beer, disinfectant and stale sweat, the sound of cursing and swearing, it was ugliness and darkness within those dark, dark houses that had been condemned a hundred years earlier. As long ago as 1837, Charles Dickens started a weekly serial called Oliver Twist which graphically described life in the slums. His writings touched the conscience of the emerging middle class, yet their vested interest in improving their infrastructure and enhancing their culture took precedence over helping the very poor.

The open countryside was beautiful, it was magnificent, the smell was of fresh air and the sound was the sweet music of birds and insects, so gentle to the ear. What a contrast it was for me. Instead of playing amongst grimy cobbled courtyards and two smelly open toilets shared by six houses and around sixty people I had the run of miles and miles of open fields, with their soft grass, tall trees, leafy bushes and abundant wildlife. I gazed open-mouthed as two powerful horses strained every muscle to pull what looked like tons of hay on a wooden cart. I filled my lungs with the fresh perfume of nature. I climbed trees instead of lamp-posts, hung around a

73

blacksmith's forge, rather than the side door of the local pub. I played innocently among the hay with children rather than kicking a tin can in a courtyard. Words cannot adequately portray such sensations. Such rich experiences have to be felt in order to be appreciated. Even the farmers who lived all their lives in the countryside could not truly empathise with what slum city-dwellers experienced when they abandoned themselves to nature for the first time. All these city-dwellers needed was the heart and imagination to be touched by the wonder of it all – Mom and Dad lacked both.

I walked to the reservoir that provided fresh water to the polluted city twelve miles away. I sucked in the fresh air and felt the wind across my face. When night fell I looked across the great expanse of water and saw a million stars reflected in it, like diamonds sparkling just for me! Then I turned my eyes upward to the sky and saw a shooting star. It was beautiful, a healing balm, and I wallowed in it.

Paradise was learning to play cricket in the open fields, jumping across wide streams, riding bareback on the farmer's retired horses, trying to catch frogs and small fish in empty jam-jars, laughing and giggling, being at one with nature. Paradise was outside 335 Stonehouse Lane. Behind its closed doors was Hell.

CHAPTER 4
THE EARLY DAYS AT 335

Chapter 4
THE EARLY DAYS AT 335

I was cold. I am always cold. Even today I complain if the heating is not right, and I hate the cold. Cold for me has a presence. It is a force that tries to penetrate my soul. I was born during one of the worst winters of the century, when heavy snow brought much of the nation to a grinding halt. The cold weather stopped me playing in the garden of Erdington Cottage Homes, which would have been such a delight compared to the dirty, smelly courtyard outside the house where we had squatted.

"Poor ragged robin. Caught in my cage. All I wanted was to feed you. But all you wanted was freedom.

Freedom is worth fighting for. Freedom is worth dying for.

Poor me! .. trying to cage you, but freedom cannot be trapped.

I wonder ... will I ever be free?"

— A Child's Thoughts

It was the blistering icy cold that hurt my face, on the day when the strange woman took me away from a Christmas that I would have enjoyed. It was her cold heart that decided that the extra week's Family Allowance, army pay and ration coupons were more important than letting her children enjoy at least one Christmas. It was a cold, snowy winter that greeted our arrival in Bartley Green at a very cold house that would be my home for the next ten years. The rooms downstairs were cold and the bedrooms were even colder. The thin blankets and various coats on the bed did not keep us warm during the bitterly cold nights that were to come. But it was my soul, my inner being, that became even colder than the temperature outside. Slowly but surely I withdrew into myself. Whenever there was an opportunity to communicate with neighbours in the street, talk to the workers on the farms or greet ramblers in the countryside, I found I could not speak. I felt paralysed. I became cold in my own isolation and a stranger to my family. Our emotions imprint lasting memories deep within us and my childhood is a huge source of cold memories.

I was unable to relate to other children or my local community. My contact with Mr and Mrs Taylor next door was always brief and occasional and with other people in the street even less so. Although I made contact with children, my relationships with them never lasted or developed, not because they didn't want them to, but because I became 'cold' towards them.

This freezing isolation, this icy indifference, this lonely existence may well have been because I was dyslexic and tongue–tied, but my memory always associates it with the external coldness that had become part and parcel of my childhood.

The winter of 1946-1947 – our first at 335 – was one of the coldest of the century. The snow was deep and much of the countryside was snowbound for two months.

> "I like the buttercup and daisy flowers in the fields. They both have bright yellow eyes looking up, but they close at night time. I feel like the field flowers. When I am out of the house something inside me opens up as I walk the fields talking to myself. When I get home at night, something inside me closes down and all I can do is hum quietly to myself."
>
> — A Child's Thoughts

At the back of our house, snow had drifted down from the farmland and was banked up against the windows. It was impossible to open our back door so we were unable to go out and explore our surroundings. My two older brothers, Donald and John, were only ten months apart in age and they had no difficulty in playing together and occupying their time. Donald was the stronger, although John was more clever. John suffered

from a lack of affection and frequent asthma attacks. He had to overcome these obstacles, which hindered him as he strove to achieve his full potential as an adult. I envied him then and I still recognise qualities in John that I lack. Bernard had just reached his fourth birthday. He played a lot with Brian who was only eighteen months old. Later Bernard had to spend three years at a convalescent hospital/school, so my younger brothers were separated at a critical time when their friendship might have developed to a deeper level. Jean was just eight and I was coming up to my sixth birthday when we moved into 335.

> "Mom and Dad don't notice me.
> Jean never speaks to me; Donald and John do sometimes. Bernard and Brian talk to each other.
> I speak but no-one listens. Most of the time, I talk to myself in my head. I think I must live inside my head. I wish I could get my thoughts out of my head."
> — A Child's Thoughts

Being a severe winter, many of the birds from the countryside had already migrated to warmer climes. Kept indoors by the weather, and with no one to play with, I gazed out of the window and saw a bird I'd never seen in the slums. It was a little red robin. I was fascinated by it. At first I threw a few pieces of bread out of the window, but because the snow was soft, the

80

bread sank too deep for the bird to reach it. In the end I put a piece of paper out to hold the bread. This was my first encounter with a robin and it was a delightful experience.

I don't know if I dreamt it or if it really happened but I felt sorry for that red robin out in the cold and so desperate for food that he kept coming to our window. I decided to catch the robin and put it in a cage. I am not sure what the trap was made from, but it was a wire frame held on a stick with a piece of string. When the little fellow came for his bread, I pulled the string and trapped him. Whether real or imaginary the image of that trapped robin influenced me greatly. The little robin flung himself from side to side in the trap, hitting himself against the frame with such incredible force that his feathers flew around the cage. After what seemed a long time, he collapsed, exhausted. I felt sorry and knew I had made a mistake. I decided to let him go. As I approached him, his eyes were wide open and glazed with fear. They met mine as if to say, 'Why did I have to endure that? What did I do to deserve being trapped?' He was so weakened and shocked that he didn't fly away immediately, even though he was free. Eventually he left, but he never came back for the bread I continued to put out for him.

For years, the trapped robin would serve as a parable to me of 335 Stonehouse Lane – my parents, my inability to express myself and to demonstrate that I had a working brain and was not a dimwit.

In the short time between our moving into 335 and Dad's return from the army mother decorated their bedroom. Was she feeling guilty for bearing a child that was not his? Or was she hoping that her efforts in the house would pacify Dad? Events later proved it was the latter.

Dad unexpectedly brought a friend with him and told Mom to move Jean out of her bedroom so that his pal could use it, but Mom refused. So the first night Dad was home he shared the double room with this man while Mom slept in the already overcrowded boys' room. In the early hours of the morning, Dad called Mom out and she was met by two naked men who desired only one thing. Mom says that she kicked the man where it hurt, but allowed Dad to 'take' her while the other man looked on. After the ordeal she went back to the boys' bedroom and in the morning she threatened she would report what had taken place to Dad's army superiors. The other man left without any comment.

This is Mom's side of the story, which she recounted on her return after twenty-eight years' absence, and it concurs with the picture that she depicted many times of Dad's behaviour and attitude to her during the first years of their marriage, before they moved to 335. She reported that she was once raped by Dad and three men. As Bernard was conceived around that time, he has often wondered whether he was a full brother or a half-brother to his siblings. Of all the children, he has grown up more like his Uncle Tom on mother's side, who, regardless of the amount he ate, hardly ever put on any weight at all.

> "I dreamed again of the red robin
> who I trapped in a cage.
> I now understand why he kept hurting himself trying to escape from the trap. I now understand why when he escaped, he never came back.
> One day, I will escape!
> One day, I will be free!"
>
> — A Child's Thoughts

The rest of us follow mother and grandmother's line and have the opposite problem of having to watch our weight.

Whether Dad went over the top with his sexual appetites, we, his children, will never know. What we do know is that when mother eventually left, the various acquaintances he brought home were of dubious character and one of them, Betty from Cardiff, was a prostitute. If, as Mom told us, Dad really was sexually depraved then it only makes her desertion of

83

the children, especially Jean, more cruel and evil, knowing that she was leaving us to his mercy (or lack of it, as subsequent events demonstrated).

Slowly, the snow began to melt away. Before long we made contact with the other children in the lane: the Cooper's, the Donnelly's, the Price's and many more. We became familiar with the names of all the occupants of the houses in our lane. To the right of us were families by the names of Golding, Cecil, Bayliss, Connelly, Cooper and Forsyth and to the left of us were neighbours by the names of Taylor, Kinchin, Martin, Hagley (who used to keep pigs), Smith (who kept chickens), Clifton, Newman, Nash, Daniels, Price, Fritz,

> "I like it when Dad tells us the stories of the war, but I can't believe that everyone else is bad but us."
>
> — A Child's Thoughts

Keys, Newland and Raymond. Next to the last house where the Raymonds lived, a pathway led to the farm and opposite was a small collection of houses where the Bishops lived. From this long list of names, it is clear that there were plenty of children for us to mix with, yet I only mixed with them occasionally and not enough to form permanent friendships. I believe this was due to my inability to speak clearly and because the development of my mind, though undisciplined, gave me thoughts and interests which simply playing

84

children's games would not satisfy. It was as though I always wanted to discover something new. My siblings were much more sociable, and before long Donald and John would become part of a little gang of children and together they would explore the farmland around us.

Across the road from us, huge bulldozers were preparing the land for new houses, although it was some years before the development took place. An isolated property which was our village shop was being converted into a larger store. Originally the shop was just one room, but the partition between the two downstairs rooms was removed to extend the premises. The nearest general store was at the top of Jiggins Lane, a walk of between one and two miles. We could take the bus which came every hour, but if we walked one stop, it only cost us one halfpenny! So we walked one way, and paid one halfpenny to return by bus when we were laden with the shopping!

The spring and summer of 1947 brought happy days, and regular visitors from the slums. It made me feel that we had become important in some way or had attained a higher status. I can remember thinking that we must have improved if people were willing to come and visit us. What I found interesting, though, was

85

"The farmer's black and white horses are strong, very strong - much stronger than the farmer. Yet they do everything the farmer tells them to do. The farmer looks very small by the side of the horses, but they never run away from him, no matter how hard they work or tired they become. I wonder what the secret of the farmer is?"

— A Child's Thoughts

that these visitors from the slums did not use the opportunity to roam around the countryside. It was as if they had eyes that could not see, ears that could not hear, and hearts that could not respond. I am sure this was not true of everyone from the slums, but it did seem to be true of many. For much less than the amount of money spent on strong drink they could have taken their children out into the open countryside on sunny days to the bluebell woods or the reservoir, all less than an hour's journey by public transport.

Not far from us was an open field where some retired horses were kept. Children tried to jump onto the horses' backs to get a free ride but without success. After a while I had the idea of dragging a bale of hay that the owners had left for the horses under a tree with an overhanging branch. I would climb onto the branch and then drop down onto the back of the horse

86

when it came over to eat the hay. My plan worked! I was able to get a few free rides, albeit only short ones, and one old horse always ran me into the side of a thorny hedge!

The farmland was criss-crossed by hedgerows and dotted with trees. In one area there was a cluster of trees and a stretch of marshland. According to local gossip a child had drowned in the marsh and his body had disappeared altogether.

Birmingham City Council had acquired several farms for redevelopment. They were allowed to go to rack and ruin while waiting for clearing work to begin in preparation for building ten thousand houses all around us. Released into the countryside from the discipline of institutions, and the claustrophobia of the slums meant our imagination was given free rein. Certainly the pictures I created in my mind and my dreams were extraordinarily vivid at this time and these derelict farms became, in our imagination, places where ghosts lived. We were often tempted to break into them. Bartley Green was the birthplace of the tallest giantess, measuring nearly eight feet in height, as recorded in the Guinness Book of Records. Born on 26 July 1895 Jane Runford was commonly known as

'Jinny'. The story went that she died on April Fools' Day in 1922 and her ghost haunted a medical museum in Birmingham University. Many years later, I discovered that her skeleton had actually been mounted and was indeed preserved in the university's medical school, that she really was seven feet and eleven inches tall, and did die on April the first! The idea of a ghost haunting a place might have come from a child's imagination but apparently, Jane Runford's skeleton has since mysteriously disappeared from the medical school!

> "It's strange to think that in our small village of Bartley Green we had the tallest lady in the world. I wonder where the tallest man is!"
> — A Child's Thoughts

Each of the terraced houses in Stonehouse Lane had its own front garden. Many of them were beautifully kept. Dad started working on the garden and Donald and John were forced to help out. In later years, all of us would be garden labourers for dad – digging, weeding, planting and cutting the grass. Bernard remembers being made to cut the grass with a pair of scissors whereas I only remember having to trim the edges of the lawn with blunt scissors! The front garden was quite small. A medium-sized tree grew in it as well as a large bush which produced the most beautiful flowers. Dad, with the help of us children, kept the lawn neat and he also planted some gladioli. As I was small the tall stems seemed to reach as high as my face with their beautiful clusters of rich, bold blooms. We had never seen anything like it in the overcrowded houses in the city. Mom and Dad even shaped out the numbers of our house in the front hedge and people passing by used to comment on the topiary, which always pleased mom.

During the early days at 335 we always had a meal together on Sundays. Although the duration of this family tradition was short-lived, the memory of those meals has stayed with us all. This was not the normal weekday food of potato mixed with corned beef or a tin of Irish stew with vegetables – this was a real roast, served with fresh vegetables. Thanks to the roast, there would be dripping which we would spread on bread for breakfast all week. It was far superior to Echo margarine which was hard and lumpy and impossible to spread evenly. We detested Echo but ate it because we were so hungry. Over the meal, Dad would mesmerise us with stories of the war, and at first it looked as though he and Mom were going to make a go of family life. Even so, Mom usually ignored us and Dad disciplined us severely if we did anything not to his liking. Fear of the army belt was a constant reality.

When dad got a job at Birmetals, a steel works two or three miles away, extra money started coming into the house. We were growing quickly and beginning to wear out the second-hand clothes given to us by the children's homes, so we were in desperate need of new clothing. But Mom and Dad did not spend the extra money on our needs. They began to leave us alone at home, insisting that we stayed in the house as they did not want the neighbours to think that we were neglected or causing a nuisance. They went to the pub or the pictures often treating themselves to a bag of chips on the way home. We children seldom had chips, although I think occasionally we were allowed to share a bag between the six of us.

Dad's work was heavy labour. He moved metal bars in and out of furnaces and sweated for his wages. He did not own a bike so he had to walk to work and back. Now that Dad was working he didn't have the time or inclination to tell us stories about his heroism in the war. He became short-tempered and woe betide us if we got under his feet. If anything displeased him, out would come his army belt from the cupboard and we would be threatened. I think we were threatened more often than we were hit, except for Donald. Donald was beginning to get out of hand. He stopped out longer than the rest of us. Not being Dad's natural son made the relationship even more difficult. At night time

John, no doubt picking up on the tension created by the shouting, arguing and physical violence generated between mother and father, had severe asthma attacks which kept us all awake at night. Sometimes he would sleep on the sofa downstairs and we would hear Dad shouting to him to turn over in the hope that he would stop coughing. Eventually, John was taken away to convalesce, a pattern that would be repeated with Bernard.

When father and mother went out, the tension went with them. Their regular trips to the Weoley Castle Picture House suited us! The picture house at Weoley Castle was one of the cheaper cinemas in the area and was about two and a half miles away. Mom and Dad went to the early film shows, so that they could go into the Weoley Castle pub afterwards. They would stay there drinking all evening and arrive back home very late. On the way home they would usually buy themselves a bag of chips. Some nights the smell of beer and greasy chips would remind me of the days we spent in the slums. Part of the slum mentality was obviously still with us, and the worst part was yet to come, for their going out was the beginning of violence rearing its ugly head at 335. This way of living – neglecting the

> "I missed the Sunday hot food today. I must go to school tomorrow, or I will die without food."
>
> — A Child's Thoughts

children and using Dad's wages in pursuit of personal pleasure – was a repetition of mother and father's former lifestyle in the slums before they were evicted and we were put into children's homes. Council house tenants did have more security and families were seldom evicted for non-payment of rent.

Before long having Sunday lunch together ceased. Dad continued to work on his garden and forced us children to help him when we wanted to be out running wild in the fields. Sunday evenings became like all the other evenings – Dad and Mom went out.

> "There was a nice song at the Children's Club at the little 'tin hut' church:
> "What can I give Him, poor as I am?
> If I were a shepherd, I would bring a lamb.
> If I were a wise man, I would do my part,
> Yet what can I give Him? Give my heart!"
>
> — A Child's Thoughts

At Bartley Green, there were three little Christian congregations: a Methodist chapel, a Gospel Hall and an attractive Anglican village church. Although mother had been educated in a convent school she never made any contact with these churches or encouraged us to go to them. Some of us did go to Sunday School for a time, acting on our own initiative and possibly because of invitations from other children. I went for a short time but felt that all the teachers were offering was words and although they talked about love, I felt it was on their terms and did not extend to 335 and what took place there.

As a child, what I heard about the church seemed to mock my life rather than help me. This does not mean that I was not thinking about God, even at a young age. In fact, I was having all kinds of thoughts. I could not comprehend why so much money was spent on those who had much and so little on those who had nothing. I considered the miracles of nature and tried to fathom out the natural instincts of the animals, birds and insects. I used to wonder what it would feel like to fly like a bird and emigrate in winter. I could not understand how God could be interested in the life of every creature but be not interested in me and my family. If God could do anything, why couldn't he do something to transform my parents into a real mother and father?

When I grew older I would walk alongside the vast expanse of the reservoir and see reflections of the heavens in the water, and I would question the meaning of life and of the universe itself – similar thoughts to those the Greek philosophers wrestled with

93

2,700 years ago.

Mom and Dad often had a bust up. If it was mild, they would simply hit one another and things would simmer down. I remember mom having an argument with Dad and throwing half a loaf of bread at him. For once he took it meekly and did not retaliate. It was difficult to understand what the arguments were about, but there were forbidden topics such as the baby Mom had had adopted and Mom's infidelity. In those early years at Bartley Green I think Dad was content with his local pubs, pictures and garden but Mom wasn't. She wanted to spend more time in the city.

> "The stars have been there from the beginning which means I can see the same stars as anybody else. This makes me the same as everybody else. I am glad!"
> — A Child's Thoughts

After a while, Dad began to complain about his back and wouldn't go into work. Many people who worked in the furnaces suffered from back trouble and took time off. For the first few weeks of sick leave, you could claim dole money which covered the basic cost of food and rent. A new phrase, 'swinging the lead', came into the English language. It described the actions of people who pretended they were sick so they didn't have to work. Mother accused Dad of 'swinging the lead' which made him furious. They argued, shouted and fought. Then came the bullying which was directed at Donald initially, but later at any of us, so that we began to fear coming home. It began to affect our schooling.

The first school I attended was opposite the parish church at the top of Bartley Green. The school buildings were Victorian and a young woman, Miss Lily Treadwell, was the headmistress. She only had one or two assistants although there must have been around 100 pupils. She was a lovely lady and never seemed to lose her temper. All the children worshipped her. Lily Treadwell was born in 1908. A failed engagement had broken her heart and she never married. Instead, she devoted herself to her pupils. At the end of each day she read us a story. Two stories stuck in my mind and I have carried them with me throughout my life.

The first story concerned a boy from a very poor family, who I thought of as me, and a girl from a well-to-do family. Both children went to boarding school. The poor boy was always getting into trouble, and was on the verge of being expelled, but the good girl defended him saving him from that fate. The boy worked hard, obtained a good job, became successful,

married the well-to-do girl and 'lived happily ever after'.

> "I dreamed today that I was a good boy and that everybody wanted to talk and to listen to me.
> I dreamed I was living in a big house with a big kitchen with lots of hot food.
> I know it was only a dream, but I liked it very much. Maybe, one day, the dream will come true! But I'm not sure."
>
> — A Child's Thoughts

The second story was about a loving father who was extremely poor but always went to work with his head held high looking at the scenery around him and whistling as he went. One day, he saw something glitter in the gutter and, stooping down, he found a sovereign which in those days was worth a fortune. The good man said to himself, 'O, what a fool I have been, spending all my time looking up and around me when I should have been keeping my eyes on the ground looking for silver sovereigns!' He started to look down into the gutter all the time. Slowly, his personality changed and he became miserable, impatient and unkind to his wife and children. One day he saw something glistening in the gutter, but when he bent down to pick it up he realised it was a little mirror. He polished it and looked into it. When he saw his sad, unshaven face he came to his senses and said to himself, 'What a greater fool I have been, to have spent so long looking in the gutter when I could have been enjoying God's creation all around me!' I must have been six years old when Miss Treadwell told that story but I've never forgotten the moral. To live for money and money alone is to have one's eyes in the gutter and one's mouth in the pigs' trough.

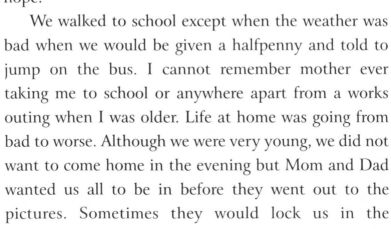

The one and only book I can remember at home was *Her Benny*. It was written by Cyril Hocking, a Liverpool author whose books were often awarded as school and Sunday School prizes. My sister Jean read the book to me. The moral teaching in the story and the way Benny overcame adversity filled me with hope.

We walked to school except when the weather was bad when we would be given a halfpenny and told to jump on the bus. I cannot remember mother ever taking me to school or anywhere apart from a works outing when I was older. Life at home was going from bad to worse. Although we were very young, we did not want to come home in the evening but Mom and Dad wanted us all to be in before they went out to the pictures. Sometimes they would lock us in the

bedroom and make dire threats if we dared leave the house. If we came in late we would get a hiding with the fearsome army belt. We lived with the dilemma of wanting to stay out for peace, yet needing to be in to avoid a beating. They tried to keep us in to stop us running wild and causing the neighbours to ask questions about what was going on. We were neglected and left to run wild and had to manage with whatever clothes we had between us. We soon learnt to put cardboard insoles into our shoes to try and cover up for the holes in the outer soles. We were constantly cutting out cardboard and knocking loose nails back in to make our feet as comfortable as possible.

On the way home from school we passed a blacksmith who still kept an old forge going. He worked his furnace by foot with the huge fire sending out a shower of sparks as he pumped the bellows. His sleeves were rolled up and his round happy face was aglow in the firelight. He always allowed us children to watch him work, especially in the winter when we could warm ourselves on the way home. He was a big strong man and though he probably had little formal education, he had no problem turning a piece of metal into a horseshoe that was exactly the right size. Each process was fascinating to watch: the long piece of metal held in the furnace and slowly bent round the oval mould, the shaping of the lip in the bow of the horseshoe, the holes for the nails (which he also made by hand) and the dipping of the glowing horseshoe into a bucket of cold water which made it bubble and steam rise. It was a fascinating and memorable sight. Today that blacksmith's shop is part of a house.

> "What a greater fool I have been, to have spent so long looking in the gutter, when I could have been enjoying God's creation all around me!"
>
> — A Child's Thoughts

It was marvellous when free milk was introduced in primary schools. Every day we had one-third of a pint of milk to drink. It was rich with cream and when there were some bottles left over those of us who were really poor were allowed a second. Miss Treadwell always seemed to give me an extra bottle. The food we ate at home lacked any sort of variety. Our main meal was usually mashed potato and corned beef or Irish stew. Sometimes mother would buy a breast of mutton. It would be boiled and boiled before she added vegetables to the greasy mess. The free meals we received at school kept body and soul together and provided us with a reasonable diet although, like at home, the food was repetitious. Children didn't want to admit they were receiving free meals at school. It labelled them as

99

the 'poorest of the poor'. It was difficult to disguise the fact, as those having free meals had to go to the second sitting. I remember how ashamed I felt when I handed the weekly coupons for free meals to the teacher. Those coupons proved to me that I had a mother and father who did not care for me properly so I was dependent on the school to take over that responsibility. For hungry children like me, the shame of free meals was offset by large servings. We came at the end of the queue and since the kitchen staff were keen to see all the food disposed of, we were offered generous second helpings without having to ask! It is strange when a child feels the tension of negative and positive emotions working against each other over one of the basic necessities of life – food.

I faced similar problems when I went to the NSPCC to get second-hand clothes which had been donated by the more well-to-do families. I was always grateful for the food and clothes, but inevitably I felt uncomfortable – a painful mix of shame and diffidence.

Occasionally there was a ray of hope in our lives. One day a second-hand piano arrived and a wireless set! Then mother acquired a new harmonica. She knew a few popular tunes and always ended her repertoire with 'God Save our Gracious King'! The king at that time was George VI. When mother was singing or playing her harmonica there was calm and with the old second-hand piano I hoped there would be music and laughter in the house. Amazingly, it was John who took to playing the piano and although I learnt one simple tune, it was not my forte. When John used to play tunes I was mesmerised. How I envied him! He seemed to have confidence, an ability to express himself and he was able to script beautiful handwriting. Because Donald was away so much in institutions we looked up to John as our natural leader. With the right encourage-ment and help, I believe he could have been successful in a creative or business way. In the film, *On the Waterfront* Marlon Brando's words, 'I could have been a contender...' express what I think John must have felt often over the years. John was handsome too! When he entered his teens all the girls took notice of him. I

> "I wish people would smile like Miss Treadwell. When she smiles at me, I am happy. When I am happy, I can smile too. When I smile at Mrs. Taylor next door, she smiles back. If Mom and Dad could smile, maybe they would be happy. I smile at them, but most times I don't think they notice me. One time, Dad said, "What are you grinning at?" as if I should not be smiling."
> — A Child's Thoughts

101

always felt left outside the magic circle created by his presence, but the simple music at home and the vibrations of my humming generated a kind of charm that soothed the mixed-up wiring of my brain.

> "I like John a lot, but I am also jealous because he can speak right and play the piano and everybody likes him. I wish somebody would like me."
> — A Child's Thoughts

So the early days at Bartley Green came to an end. In those early days, I recognised Donald's strength as he stood his ground against a group of boys and John's many talents. Jean was caught up in a world of her own, playing with miniature furniture. Bernard and Brian made friends with children their age. I was well into my sixth year and still a loner. Soon another Christmas would come – our second Christmas together as a family. It came and it passed us by. This time there was not even an orange, apple or the sweets of the previous year. The three little churches had special services including items for children, but the Hicks' were not there.

Before that Christmas came Guy Fawkes night. We built a bonfire on the green verge in front of our house, although we didn't know if it was allowed. Once it was ablaze, all the neighbours came out. They cooked potatoes at the edge of the fire and shared drinks with one another. It was a very special time for me. For most of the year we were viewed as vagabonds but that evening we did something that the neighbours enjoyed. No doubt we reminded some of the adults of their own childhood.

In that first year mother did make some effort at home making. Jean remembers her planning and starting to make each of us a nightgown to keep us warm at night. She promised to sew each child's initials on them. Only one or two were actually made, and as I was the fourth child, I missed out. Mother's resolution to make a fresh start was already wearing thin. The small downstairs room, that was never used, was cleaned out and she started to decorate it, but the job was never finished, and the room was never furnished. That year my parents 'cancelled' Christmas. They simply ignored our birthdays. We did not know when our birthdays were. The day would simply come and go without recognition or mention. Except for the occasional visit of relatives from the slums, there was nothing worth looking forward to at 335 – no Christmas, no birthday parties, no family occasions, no football games with dad, no family visits to the bluebell woods or to discover the countryside together, no being a family. No wonder I felt a stranger in my own home. As long as we were out and about we could minimise the misery of being at home. But a storm was brewing and mother was the cause.

> "Can it be true?
> Mom and Dad have left the slums, but the slums have not left them.
> Now they have the open fields, yet the smelly pub is where they are at home.
> Now they have living streams, but no desire to discover them.
> Now they could take their children for walks and adventures but instead they shut the children in the house while they go to the pub and the pictures.
> Now they have the very best that creation could offer: a big new world for them, but they don't want it!
> Why? I wonder, why?"
> — A Child's Thoughts

So the early days at Bartley Green came to an end. Mother desperately missed the lifestyle that she had temporarily left behind in the city. She was more interested in going out than in looking after us. Jean and Bernard needed simple medical attention for the squints in their eyes. It was available free of charge. Bernard, Brian and myself had speech problems. Brian and I required just an initial visit to the doctor to secure the help that would have released us from years of internal torment. John and Bernard suffered from asthma. They should have lived in a stable and relaxed environment, but our home life was the very opposite, especially when the call from the city proved irresistible to mother.

CHAPTER 5
TROUBLE BREWING

I never wanted to kiss or be kissed, to hug or be hugged, by my mother. Once, she wanted me on her lap when her sister came

> "Why is it that the spider spinning a web is more interesting than anything that takes place at '335'?"
> — A Child's Thoughts

to the house and I knew it was not for my benefit, but to convey a message to her sister: 'Look! I care and I am looking after the children after all.' There were times that I smelt her presence and each time I felt nauseous. Mother's smell was not due to lack of hygiene – she always kept herself clean and tidy. Nor was it the smell of cheap perfume. It was a smell that perhaps only I could sense. It represented her relationship with me.

I longed for a mother like the lady in the Homes who appeared to me in my dreams. Later I met a similar mother figure who worked for the NSPCC and there were certain dinner ladies at school who had love left over for the waifs and strays like myself who

107

devoured the canteen food like hungry dogs.

No matter what difficulties families face, a mother's love should be the last thing to fail, not the first. Thankfully, most mothers have a strong, lasting love for their offspring. My mother knew that the life she was living away from the family would end in a crisis of such gigantic proportions that it would impact drastically on us all. She was too intelligent not to realise the consequences of her actions. The fact that she deliberately planned to leave us for good, simply demonstrates to me her lack of motherliness.

I was not important to my mother. I learnt that it was best for her to have me out of her sight and out of her mind. What happened to me was of little consequence to her. I was insignificant. So, no kisses. No hugs. No closeness. No normality. No mother or mother figure, which is surely the birthright of every child who comes into this world. When I cried silently, she never heard the struggling of my soul: 'Why, mother? Why couldn't you simply be a mother? Why did I become afraid of you, unsure of you, insecure in your presence? What, mother, made me feel as if I had no existence as far as you were concerned? What made me feel that my only need of you was for protection from my father, or to have your coat as an extra blanket in the cold winter nights? Was I ugly? Was I bad? Was I so deformed, so silent, so 'nothing' that there was no meaningful contact between us?'

Mother was not happy at home. She had been looking for a reason to go back into the city to work again with her friends in a factory called Lindons which specialised in spraying bicycle lamps and parts for other factories. Maybe some of the arguments that took place at home were because Mom was constantly saying that she needed to go back to Lindons to earn extra money. Before long mother was not only working through-out the week, but on Saturdays too. The extra money bought mother new clothes while our ragged coverings went from bad to worse. She also started coming home later each day saying she had had to do additional work. It meant that we were at Dad's mercy on Saturdays as well in the evenings and in the school holidays.

One Saturday Mr Taylor gave me a bucket and told me to collect the horse manure that a local horse had deposited on the road. He wanted it for his garden and

> "The teacher keeps telling me to get my hair cut. I keep telling my Mom, but she never listens. When a letter came from the teacher, Mom put a basin over my head and cut my hair around it using her own spittle to control the hair. Now I know why they call it a 'basin cut'. My hair feels funny so short. It won't be cut again for a long time."
>
> — A Child's Thoughts

109

"I went to the 'Saturday Matinee' for the first time today and was surprised to see how many children were there. The picture house was full! The children sang lots of songs I had never heard before. Hop Along Cassidy was the hero of the film and he could always outshoot the bad men, even when riding fast on his horse.
I hope I will become a cowboy one day."

— A Child's Thoughts

he gave me a halfpenny for it. Then he asked if I would like to take two buckets and collect manure from the field where the retired horses grazed. I did, and sometimes I managed to collect four or six bucketfuls which earned me enough to go to the Saturday matinee at the pictures. If the manure had dried out it took longer to fill the bucket and I can remember having to wait for the horses to produce more for me! Dad soon made me fetch manure for him but without payment of course. My response was to part–fill the bucket with straw and when I emptied it on Dad's patch, he didn't realise that he was only getting half as much as Mr Taylor! Years later John told me that he and Donald had also collected manure for dad. On one occasion Donald gave the horses Beechams pills, a laxative to encourage them to deposit the manure faster!

The Saturday matinee cost one penny and a

halfpenny and sometimes I was able to take Bernard and Jean with me. I must confess that usually I was not that generous and I went on my own. The number of children who went to the matinee was amazing. Two or three hundred of us were entertained before the films were shown and we all joined in singing popular songs such as *Roll out the Barrel, I've got a Lovely Bunch of Coconuts!* and *Bobby Shaftoe's Gone to Sea.* There was a main film, various short ones, and trailers which encouraged the children to return with their parents in the evening.

We loved films about cowboys and Indians even though the storyline was always the same. Afterwards we would run from the pictures in various directions, pretending to be Indians by putting our hands over our mouths to make the 'haw-haw-haw' sound. I remember watching Hop-along Cassidy in serial form. One episode ended with him facing twelve men. Was this the end of Hop-along Cassidy? Surely he couldn't outgun twelve men? I made sure I went the following week and I couldn't wait until the main feature. All I wanted to know was whether Hop-along Cassidy had survived! Needless to say he not only routed the complete dozen, but he shot their guns out of their hands! In those innocent films, no one ever seemed to get killed. They all got up and appeared in later episodes! Jean Autrey, Roy Rogers and an aged Clark Kent, who played Superman, and another superhero called Marvel were memorable stars from my time at the Saturday matinees. If I had no money to go to the pictures, I went to a door at the side entrance. A little chip of wood had been carved out with a screwdriver and if I put my left eye to the hole, I was able to see about twenty per cent of the screen. I used to watch as much as I could and I became adept at working out the plot! Skimping and saving the pennies for the pictures became a major pastime for me and no doubt I found the films a crude kind of education which stimulated my imagination.

Life at home was going from bad to worse. One Sunday father and mother had a huge row. Mother had the stronger will both mentally and verbally so Dad ended up retaliating physically. This time the fighting got completely out of hand. It was so bad that mother told me to call the police. A telephone box had been installed just outside the local village store, so I ran and called 999. By the time the police came, the fight was over. I got hundreds of beatings from dad over the years, because I had called the police that day.

Already a loner, I began to sink deeper

into myself. The months rolled into seasons and the seasons rolled into years, but there was no improvement in our situation. Before long, Donald was in trouble for something petty. Middle-class society did not know how to deal with working-class kids, especially those who had recently come from the slums. Because working-class kids did things not dreamt of by those in higher classes, the offences seemed worse than

> "The 'Pictures' fill my mind with so many ideas and help me forget home. I know it's not real. The films are like my dreams, but I like them.
> Maybe, one day, I will have a horse. Maybe, one day, I will ride away and go anywhere I want to. Maybe, one day, I will be somebody."
> — A Child's Thoughts

they truly were and the punishments inflicted reflected their perception rather than the reality. Donald was put on probation, which meant that from time to time the probation officer would come to the house. Dad insisted that the house was spotlessly clean in case the probation officer came. He wanted to be thought of as a good father, and he was always charming when visitors were present. While Mom was at work and Dad alternated between periods at work and on the dole, we children cleaned the house.

The ritual for cleaning the main room was to move the furniture into the spare room then clean out the

113

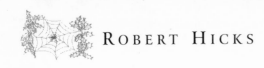

cast-iron grate, which also involved trying to catch the tiny silverfish which were always around! Then we had to get on our hands and knees and wash and polish the lino. Finally we would bring the furniture back in and dust. Once the lino was polished, we dared not go back in the room for fear of leaving shoe prints on the shiny surface. If we did have to go back into the room we would put pieces of paper down to walk on to avoid getting a beating.

> "Jean looks funny.
> Bernard looks funny.
> Brian speaks funny.
> I speak funny. But it's not funny. It's not fair.
> Why can't we just be normal the same as everyone else?"
>
> — A Child's Thoughts

I am not sure how old I was when I began to use the box which covered the gas meter in the corner of the main room as a desk. Wedged in that corner, I would copy out words and read whatever comics I had managed to acquire. What I mean by 'read' is that, apart from a few words, I would make up the stories myself based on the cartoon pictures. Many years would pass before I was able to read and write, but eventually I would write real words in that same corner.

Mom would sometimes come home very late. Her excuse was that either she had worked overtime or had called at her mother's on the way home. Dad used to line us up and question us. He had his belt in his hand

114

and occasionally used it if any of us said the wrong thing. His interrogations were always about mother and her behaviour. The house was becoming a place of fear and we children knew of no logical reason to justify it.

Jean and Bernard both suffered from an optical defect which made them cross-eyed. They faced ridicule at school because of their condition. Jean, in particular, was deeply hurt by this. Not only was she having problems at home, but now at school as well. Jean believed her eye problems started when her flimsy nightgown caught fire as she tried to get warm by the open gas oven. She was rushed to hospital with severe burns, but it seems that the trauma of seeing the flames engulf her seems to have weakened her eyes at that stage. It would take a long time for the burns to heal and many years for the scars to fade. The more I reflect on Jean, the greater my pride in her grows even though she would be the first to confess that she made many wrong choices in her own life.

115

Neither mother nor father showed any concern about Jean and Bernard's eye problems. They were equally indifferent to John's mild asthma attacks, only bothering when his attacks became so severe that the whole family thought he was dying. We

boys had to get used to his coughing and gasping for breath as we shared a bed in a small room. We were powerless to help him.

What did concern mother and father were the periodic visits from the probation service. Dad and Mom's behaviour was amazingly transformed whenever the probation officer came round to check on Donald. They pointed out the difficulties of bringing up a family of six young children and said they were doing their best. When the probation officer saw that the house was clean, he seemed satisfied and no doubt filed a good report.

We did receive some help from outside agencies. Our parents managed to obtain free meals for us all, as well as second-hand clothes from the NSPCC. Every item of clothing was too large so that we would grow into it. My shoes were far too big for me and by the time my feet grew to fit them properly, the soles were leaving the uppers because of the way I had shuffled to try and keep them on! For a time I tied them together with a piece of string. I wore short trousers until I was fifteen. The free meals meant that when we went to school we didn't have to beg and steal from other children, although I can remember days when I would go an entire day without food. In the evening I would ravenously devour whatever was available as fast as I could before Donald dipped his finger into my plate and stole any of it.

Dinners were one of the best things about school. Scholastically, the only subject in which I excelled was maths. I understood some of the other subjects, too, but I could not express my knowledge or write answers down in a presentable way. If it had not been for my maths, I would have been in the bottom form and bottom of the class. My maths enabled me to be top of my class, despite the many days I played truant. On paper the school rated me as a 'hopeless case, having no natural or acquired ability' and saw no future for me. I was excluded from the extra work done with children after school and I was never even approached about holiday adventures and trips.

I played truant on the days there were exams or when I knew the subject would embarrass me. I liked

> "Tiger, the cat, had kittens in my bed in the night. She came to me because I am her friend and I hum and she purrs to me. Dad drowned all the kittens in the morning because we have no food for them. I keep crying in my heart. Only Tiger hears me. She looks so sad and has stopped purring and now cries in 'miaows' for her lost kittens. Dad has told me I must not let Tiger come in the house again - but I will."
> — A Child's Thoughts

117

school, but the teachers did not know how to handle children like me. I would run to the wide open spaces, to the fields and streams where I always felt accepted and was never made to feel foolish. Once I played truant for such a long period that it ran into weeks rather than days. I don't know how I survived without school meals, but some of Dad's food went missing!

The years rolled by. At first mother came home from work on the five o'clock bus. John and the younger children eagerly awaited her arrival I would be out wandering in the fields. Gradually, however, mother started working late so John rarely saw her. Then there were times when she didn't come home at all. She tried to pacify Dad by saying that she was staying at her mother's and, although her mother would have backed up the story, she was actually having an affair with a West Indian who had a family of his own in the West Indies. We saw less and less of Mom, and the atmosphere at home went from bad to worse, and from worse to dreadful. Sometimes two or three days would pass before mother came home. If Dad was

> "I wish I could stop dreaming of running around looking for food and only wearing a short shirt. I wish Dad and Mom were not always in my dreams eating my food. I don't like night time."
>
> — A Child's Thoughts

not working at Birmetals he would spend the morning in bed, rising early in the afternoon to work in the garden and then go out in the evening drinking, with or without mother. We children were neglected, but our lifestyle at 335 had its routine. Each morning we washed ourselves in cold water at the kitchen sink and ate a breakfast of bread toasted over the gas stove flame, spread with Echo margarine. Occasionally we had porridge made with water. Some of the others seasoned it with salt, but I could not eat it like that. If we were very fortunate we were able to have a little milk on the porridge which made it palatable.

The journey to school was over two miles. Only too often I would have to collect Dad's newspaper first, which meant walking an extra two miles. This always made me late for school and I would be caned.

After the war many teachers were called back out of retirement. One of them was Mr Woolley, my maths teacher, who seemed to spend most of his time working in the school gardens. Once, he wrote up on the blackboard a set of sums taken from his textbook. For the next forty minutes we were expected to work out the answers. Within a few minutes, I knew all the answers as I saw them clearly in my mind without having to work them out, so I put up my hand. At first, he was puzzled. He could not believe that I had completed the page with correct answers. Then it

dawned on him that I must have taken his book and extracted the answers from the back of it. If he had

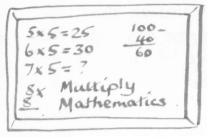

thought about it more deeply, he would have realised that as I did not know which sums he was going to put on the board, I would have had to copy out the answers from the entire book.

However, Mr Woolley was convinced he was right and tried to force me to confess that I had cheated. I kept shaking my head from left to right. Eventually he took out the dreaded cane. Not only had I cheated, but now I was lying too. Not only was I lying, I was also obstinate. He told me to put out my hand. I refused. I had been given six of the best more than once. Standing up to Mr Woolley's accusation for something I had not done, sowed a seed of steely determination within me that one day I would have to use in a confrontation with my father.

'Bobby, put your hand out!' Mr Woolley repeated. I refused. 'You put your hand out now, or you will get more than you bargained for!' I refused. Mr Woolley found himself cornered. He was locked into a battle of wills in front of all the children in the classroom. His face got redder and redder and part of me wanted to put out my hand for his benefit but I still refused. In the end he told the class to continue working while he took me to the headmaster. The headmaster, Mr Humphries, was a big powerful man. I stood before him, a boy dressed in rags who hadn't washed properly for days, with dirty, long scruffy hair and who was accused of cheating and refusing to take his punishment. To the best of my ability, I explained to Mr Humphries that I knew the answers to those sums and to many other things as well, but I could not always write them down. He gave me a puzzled look and then he took an arithmetic book from his cupboard and picked out various sums for me to do. He gave me a pencil and I was expected to give instant answers in front of him! My mind was not clear but I could see most of the answers and although some were not completely right, the exercise persuaded Mr Humphries and Mr Woolley that I had not been lying. I did not get the cane. Neither did I get any apology! Saddest of all, neither teacher

> "I am good at Maths in school. I am always at the top of the class. The teacher said I am good enough to be top of the school. I can 'see' the answers without a lot of thinking. Is it because I am thinking all the time? I like Maths, but I wish I could read as well. I can work out numbers easily, but I cannot understand alphabet letters. I do not understand why."
>
> — A Child's Thoughts

121

acknowledged that I had a particular mental ability that needed to be developed and fostered. I went back into the classroom and to the same old routine in which my mind stayed trapped within my head.

One thing did change – Mr Woolley treated me with more respect after that incident. Post-war schools like mine, situated amongst newly-built housing estates struggled with way above average class sizes. I am not sure how many children were in my class, but there were probably over fifty. At the end of each school day one teacher would read us a serial story. The story was *Midshipman Easy and Ready*, a tale of adventures in exotic and exciting places. It filled my mind and fed my imagination. How I longed to read books like that for myself! But reading was difficult for me and at that time I could only manage second-hand comics.

Life away from school was only tolerable because we could escape into the countryside that surrounded us. Most of the boys belonged to gangs, and from time to time two gangs would meet on opposite sides of the fast-

> "Why can I not speak what is in my mind? When the teacher speaks, I understand. When he gives me books to read and write in, I don't.
> I wish he would speak more and not give me the books, but I do like looking at the pictures in them."
>
> — A Child's Thoughts

122

flowing stream and throw stones at each other in order to drive their opponents back. Whichever side had the larger gang on the day inevitably won. I can't remember anyone ever getting hurt by the stones – obviously, it was a ritual! One gang had a large bulldog on their side. Our gang had Lassie and sometimes a dog called Prince. We decided to push the bulldog and Lassie into the water in the hope that they would fight for the right teams, but Lassie was not having any of it and ran back home soaking wet!

One of our favourite places was the old oak tree. It had been struck by lightning which had burnt a cavity in the trunk large enough for children to squeeze in. Over a period of time the dead wood from inside had been chipped out and it became our den. It was also known as 'the lovers' oak', although I never witnessed any lovers there, so presumably any loving that took place was in secret and probably in the dark of night! With the oak tree, the fields and woodland, we felt like Robin Hood and his merry men. Our imagination knew no bounds and we invented all kinds of games and pastimes. We saved empty baked beans tins, gouged rough vents in the sides and attached a piece of

123

string. We filled the can with sticks, pushed in a chunk of turf for a lid and lit the wood with a match. Then we swung the cans round and round by the string so that the circulating air would make the flames burn fiercely within the can. When we heard that the French ate frogs' legs, we caught a large frog, killed it and cooked its legs on a 'fire can'. But everyone refused to eat them and our perception of the French nation went down as a result of the exercise!

The old oak tree was where Bernard, Brian and I made plans to go scrumping in the orchard next to the farmer's house. It was a dangerous exercise and we had never attempted it before! When it was dusk we set off crossing two fields before we reached the orchard, which was protected by a hedge and a wire fence. We pulled up the wire fence and channelled out the earth below to make enough clearance for us to scramble underneath. Bernard climbed a pear tree and started throwing some of the fruit down to us. We were putting the fruit into our pockets when a light suddenly came on in the house. We all froze. There was a young girl's face at the window. The farmer's daughter was looking straight at us. We didn't move, but when the curtains closed and the dogs started barking we decided to scarper! I knew it would take time to scramble back under the fence, so I decided to try my luck at getting over it. I jumped and just about cleared it. Brian, who was immediately behind me, followed suit. He made it but tore his trousers in the process. We ran through the cornfields in zigzag fashion and I suspect we cost the farmer more by damaging his corn than we did by trying to steal his fruit. We must have run some distance but eventually we made our way back very timidly to the old oak tree, wondering whether the farmer and Bernard, who had not followed us, would be there ahead of us. Bernard was there! He had a cheeky grin on his face and began whistling as we approached. We could not believe it! He had stashed a pile of apples and pears inside the old oak

"I am late again for school. Dad made me go up Jiggins Lane to get his newspaper first.
The paper is called The Mirror. The first time I went for it, I thought I was getting a new mirror for the wall to replace the cracked one Dad uses for shaving. The man at the shop insisted that Dad wanted the newspaper. He was right. Dad did not tell me off for bringing a newspaper instead of a mirror, but they caned me at school for being late."
— A Child's Thoughts

125

tree. The farmer was so intent on chasing Brian and me that he had forgotten to look up into the tree where Bernard was hanging on silently! While the farmer gave chase, Bernard simply helped himself to the fruit and calmly made his way back to the oak tree. The next morning we all had tummy ache from eating too much unripe fruit! When the farmer next saw us, he held us firmly by our ears and told us in no uncertain terms that he knew we were the culprits and if we wanted any fruit we should knock on the door and ask.

In the autumn, when we were on holiday from school, we would dig up the farmer's potatoes, swedes and carrots intending to take them home and cook them. Often we were so hungry we ate them raw. We always put any flowers and stalks we had picked back in the earth to hide our handiwork. What the farmer thought when he discovered our visits, I leave to your imagination.

We took cooking apples from a neighbour's trees and baked them on a fire made out of bits of wood. One day, Dad was so hungry that he encouraged us to go scrumping, but on other occasions

> "Today, I pulled some of the farmer's carrots out of the ground to eat.
> I put the green tops back into the soil but I don't think they will grow again. I hope he won't mind me having the carrots, as I am so hungry."
> — A Child's Thoughts

126

when he found out that we had
disgraced him, he gave us a belting.
There were various allotments not far
from home. During the war years
they had been used to produce 'Food
for the Nation' but were now left
untended. On one of the allotments
was a huge damson tree. As soon as we
discovered it we decided to make a
den under its massive branches which
bent low to the ground and suited our
needs perfectly. We fitted our den out with wooden
boxes, a few candles and various bits and pieces. One
day we found a bomb that looked gigantic, although
really it was only small. I helped the others to drag the
bomb to our den. We made a shrine and swore by the
death of all in the family that we would keep the bomb
secret, but somehow the secret got out. A few days later
a policeman cycled over to our house and asked me
whether the story of the bomb was true. So much for
the covenant we had made between us. You never lied
to a policeman. The policeman made a telephone call
and before long an army truck arrived and the bomb
was disposed of unceremoniously. As to the hand
grenade we found – I believe we threw that into the
water at the bottom of a pit.

Although not many bombs had been dropped near

127

Bartley Green during the war, there was one area where bombs had left massive craters. The deep holes were full of dirty water, and little fish which we called tiddlers swam around the edges. Many children used to swim in this water, including Donald and Leslie (mother's young brother who was Donald's age) until tragically one child drowned there. We called this area the 'clay pits'. Various companies and individuals dumped their waste and rubbish there, including a considerable amount of empty bullet shells. We used these bullet shells to make arrowheads for our makeshift bows and arrows. We were, in effect, making potentially lethal weapons, though mercifully there is no story of anyone getting seriously hurt by them. I think this had more to do with the weakness of the bow than the potential danger carried by the arrows.

A few miles away from Stonehouse Lane was a natural spring where the water was always the same temperature. The cold, pure water was a sheer pleasure to drink. At one time there were many farms in the area, but by the time we moved to Bartley Green most of the farm buildings were derelict. The farm behind our house, Nonesuch Farm, was famous in local folklore because it was said that Charles II spent a night there when he was fleeing from the Battle of Worcester in September 1651. Cromwell's

Roundheads came to the farm and forced the owner to swear an oath that Charles was not there. The owner swore 'Nonesuch is here!' Good story that it is, there are no historical facts to back it up. We were exploring a derelict farmhouse one day only to discover that one of the rooms was in use. There was a bed on the floor and it was evident that someone had made the place his home. We wondered whether to steal one or two of his possessions, but decided it was wrong to rob a homeless person. I did take a pack of playing cards which were lying in one corner of the room, but I felt guilty about it for a long, long time. Indeed I still feel a sense of guilt because I stole a pack of cards from a lonely man who may have depended on playing *Patience* to pass the time away.

At another farm, which was a working farm, a gang from the bottom of Stonehouse Lane had made an entrance into the barn through a disused pigsty. The barn was stacked with hay. It had two storeys inside, the upper one being small and high up at the top of the barn.

"The old oak tree is full of mystery and secrets. Its heart is big enough for three of us and I like to hide inside it or climb up into its branches and see a long way off."

— A Child's Thoughts

129

The gang decided to climb a rope in order to reach the second storey. All the other boys could climb ropes, but

> "New clothes for just one day! I am not surprised to lose them. The big surprise was to have them at all."
>
> — A Child's Thoughts

I had never done so. The first time, they helped me to climb but the second time they left me at the bottom and told me I would only learn by doing it on my own! I tried and tried, but to no avail, so I looked around the barn instead. Suddenly I heard dogs barking, so I quickly hid behind some boxes in the corner. When the farmer opened the door, the first place the dogs ran to was the boxes. I was scared. The farmer called the dogs off, pulled me out by the ear and told me to stand by the open door. Then he called the boys down. At first everything was quiet, but slowly, one by one, the boys began to descend the rope. The dogs became very excited, barking and jumping up. Seeing that the farmer and the dogs were distracted, I decided to run for it. I ran and ran until I was totally out of breath. A short time later I heard the boys as they came across the field. They were laughing and whistling. When they caught up with me I looked at them sheepishly, being unsure about whether I should have run away or stayed. The farmer had clipped each one of them across the ear and warned them not to break into the barn again. The boys decided to expel me from their gang because I was too small, too scared and had not paid my halfpenny fee!

Although I was a bit disappointed, it did not concern me greatly because I knew I couldn't keep up with them anyway.

Around this time mother involved me in an act of deception. It was the one and only time mother chose to take me out with her in my entire life. Lindons the place where Mom worked, held an annual outing to a place called Bellevue. It was a poor man's theme park in Manchester. Mom could have taken Dad but looking back I realised that she did not want Dad to go. Indeed, she didn't want Dad anywhere near Lindons, even though sometimes he would hang around to see if he could catch Mom with any of the men who worked there.

For the outing I was given a suit to wear as well as a pair of pumps, a new shirt and some underpants – something I seldom wore. When I put the suit on, I noticed that there was a proper crease in the short trousers. The zipper jacket was big on me. I assumed this was so that I could grow into it. In the winter, I wore a woollen jumper in place of a coat or jacket unless a charity provided a coat. I was thrilled by the novel experience of putting on a new coat, fastening the zip for the first time and pulling it up to my neck. It felt strange. After the outing, it went to the pawn shop and later I discovered that the new clothes were not for my benefit. Mom was smartly dressed in a

131

recently acquired black and white check coat which we used as an extra blanket when it was cold at night. She looked attractive in it and she paid a park photographer to take a picture of her and myself together at Bellevue. I still have a copy of the photograph which she intended to use as evidence of our happy mother and son outing in her attempt to deceive Dad. None of us was ever allowed to go on school trips, so it seemed strange that mother had chosen me to go on this outing. It did not seem fair either and I would much rather have gone on a school trip. But I was excited since it was my first and only excursion outside Bartley Green for years although I felt sorry that the rest of the family was not coming. Dad insisted that if mother was going on the trip, one of the family must go with her. It was his way of ensuring there would be no opportunity for her to be with another man.

132

The day before we went on the trip, mother cut my long hair and combed it. We sat together on the coach journey to Manchester. I was by the window and Mom talked to various people nearby especially to a black man who was on his own. During the journey she told me that she felt sorry for the man on his own and asked whether I would mind if she went to talk to him. I thought she would be gone for a few minutes but she was away for a long time. When she came back she did not want to talk to me. Except for commenting on what I saw through the window, we seldom talked.

> "I wanted to feel special having time alone with my Mom for a day's outing. But now the day has come, I don't feel special. She doesn't want to talk to me. She wants to talk to a strange man."
>
> — A Child's Thoughts

The coach stopped in a small town for a refreshment break. I wanted a cup of tea, as did some of the ladies on the coach, but no one knew where to find the tea shop. I thought I had seen a cafe as we approached and I said so. For some reason, everybody was amazed when I mentioned this and Mom claimed that I was psychic rather than observant. After Mom had had a cup of tea with me, she went and had a drink with the West Indian man as well. By the end of the day I had every reason to believe mother was doing something terribly, terribly wrong.

Eventually we arrived at Bellevue. I was bewildered by the flashing lights and colours, the frenetic movement of the rides and what seemed like thousands and thousands of people jumping on and off them. I saw a girl holding a stick with what looked like a great

133

mass of cotton wool. She was eating it! It was the first time I'd seen candy floss. There were stalls all over the place and people were buying all kinds of knick-knacks and gifts.

> "I saw Mom kiss and cuddle a tall black man on the coach coming back from her Works' Outing. I know Mom will leave us one day. She doesn't love Dad or us. She only wanted me with her on the outing so that Dad would not know she was with this man. I saw so many people happy today, including my Mom. I am not happy."
>
> — A Child's Thoughts

Mother kept trying to persuade me to go on the big wheel but I was a bit scared. In the end I gave in and she reassured me that she'd be waiting for me when the ride finished. When it was over she wasn't there. When I finally found her she was talking to the same man she'd been talking to on the coach. Throughout the day he always seemed to be near us and we kept bumping into him. I didn't realise that Mom's plan was not working out. She thought I'd be fully occupied going on the swings, roundabouts and all the rides, whereas I was more than happy to look around and take it all in. Our coach party met up to have a meal together. The black man sat at a different table from us, but mother still went over to talk to him at the end of the meal. She was giving every ounce of her attention to a man who was a stranger to me. I felt left out and resentful. This was my first time in a theme park and I wanted to enjoy it but my mother wasn't interested in me. Even as a ten-year-old child I knew I was being used.

When it was time for us to go home we boarded the coach. My mother tried to encourage me to sleep, even though I wanted to look out of the window. She got me to lie across the seat and I closed my eyes and listened to what was going on. On the pretext that I was stretched across her seat as well my own she moved to sit next to the black man.

Every now and then I would open my eyes and see what they were doing. At first they were talking. Then he was kissing Mom and moving his hand over her breasts. I could not believe it! I simply stared. Although I was too young to know what was happening they seemed to be kissing for a long time. When Mom turned to look towards me, I closed my eyes quickly, then after a moment peeped again. They were kissing again. At home, Mom never kissed, hugged or acted in the way she was behaving on that coach. She was the mother of seven children and I was old enough to know that what I was witnessing was unbelievable and disturbing. I had felt rejected before this so-called 'special day'. Now I was seeing my mother displaying an ability to show love and affection to a stranger. At that moment something inside me died. It was hope. Hope was no longer a part of my feelings as far as my family was concerned. Suddenly, I heard Mr Watson call Mom. He used her nickname, Win. 'Win! Be careful, Bobby's not asleep!'

I closed my eyes, too afraid to look again. It had not been a special day for me. I had been provided with a new suit and a new pair of shoes but mother was just using me as cover in order to be with this man from the West Indies – a man who never looked me in the eye, never smiled at me, never spoke to me. For many years his face would haunt me in my dreams. He deprived me of my mother whose face I had great difficulty in recollecting. Years later, the only way I could remember what she looked like was by getting out the picture taken in Bellevue.

Mom and I were dropped off not far from home. We walked in the dark for the rest of the way as we had missed the bus. When we got in Dad was fast asleep. All the children had obviously gone through some ordeal and poor Donald was black and blue all over. Mom went berserk. She threatened to call the police. Whenever they had a row she always threatened Dad with the police, knowing he was scared of getting into trouble with them. Something must have happened in his past and he did not want to come to the notice of the authorities.

My day out had come to an end and I felt cheated. Mom had not only used me but by not reporting Dad for his cruel treatment of Donald, she was using my brother too. If she had acted in Donald's interests that day, maybe he would not have ended up in a Reform School before he joined the army. Little did I know that, very soon, we children would go from the frying pan into the fire.

Mother was pregnant again, most probably not by Dad. This set in motion the cycle that had often been repeated in the past. It was as though there was a destructive programme within my parents' marriage and the start button kept being pressed. We are not certain who the father of the child was but as her natural children we find it hard to believe that she would abandon us to a man whose violence would go from bad to worse, unless she had some real reason for doing so.

A new, sad and evil period was opening up before us and we had nowhere to run.

> "I am ten now but I never get new clothes to keep. One day Mom did get me new clothes that I thought were for me to keep. I wore the suit to go with Mom on her Works' Outing a long way away."
> — A Child's Thoughts

137

CHAPTER 6
A FAMILY ADRIFT

CHAPTER 6
A FAMILY ADRIFT

Mother began to stay out until late at night, and sometimes all night. She told us that she was working overtime to get extra money for us, and when it was too late for the last bus home she was stopping overnight at her mother's or with friends. She was earning extra money but the home and family were not benefiting from it. Her mother and sister were convinced that she was having an affair with the West Indian chap. I realised

"The river runs fast. I throw in various sticks for a race. The fastest sticks sometimes get stuck, then the slowest one wins! But in time, they all disappear.

My brothers and sisters are slowly disappearing. Drifting away, like the sticks. Sometimes they get stuck on the way, but they are still drifting and disappearing.

Sometimes, I am the only one left behind and I wonder why."

— A Child's Thoughts

141

> "Donald ran away again and now he is in trouble and we are told we will not see him for a long, long time, if ever.
> It's not his fault! It's Mom and Dad's fault!
> Why haven't we got a proper Mom and Dad?
> It isn't fair that I won't see Donald again."
>
> — A Child's Thoughts

something was going on, but I kept my thoughts and feelings to myself.

Dad didn't know what time mother came home because he went to the pub or pictures every evening and left us children alone, sometimes locked in the bedroom. In time, we learnt how to escape and roamed around the houses and fields as night fell.

Donald had been sent to Borstal and he didn't come back home again because he was called up to join the Forces and he made the army his career. Dad refused to accept responsibility for Donald's need of correction, but the way my father treated him forced him to stay away from home. Mother was living the life she wanted to lead so Donald had no one to turn to. Eventually he ran into the powerful arms of the law and was severely punished for his petty crimes, while the unending and momentous crime of which he was the victim, along with the rest of us, went undetected.

Sometimes mother came back in the evenings and claimed to have been in the house longer than was true. Dad would come home in the early hours of the morning after the pubs closed and if mother was not in the house, all Hell would break loose. We would be woken and ordered down from our bed into the kitchen and would have to stand in a line while he interrogated us.

'Where's your mother?'

'Why hasn't she come home?'

'Did she come home?'

'Did she bring anyone with her?'

'Was there a black man with her?'

'Did she talk of a Mr Palmer?'

'You must know where she is! Tell me, or I'll have to get the belt!'

'If you tell me where she is I won't hurt you.'

Roused from deep sleep and being forced to undergo this questioning was humiliating. We soon learnt to stand perfectly still, unflinching, trying not to breathe, while Dad moved up and down the line. Whoever was nearest to him at any given time might get a smack across the ears or a slap on the side of the face. When mother was at home, we begged her not to stop out at night because of the unjust treatment we would receive.

Ever since my day out with Mom, when I had witnessed her intimacy with Mr Palmer, I knew trouble was brewing. I thought that Dad would find out one day and hurt her so badly that she would end up in hospital or even dead. Whatever my thoughts and however deep my feelings were, they were locked inside me and would escape and torment me at night.

> "Mom has stopped cooking a dinner on Sundays and she spends most of her time back in the city.
> I don't know if I really miss her, but I know something terrible is going to happen."
>
> — A Child's Thoughts

As I write this book, with the advantage of many years of reflection, I still find both my parents a mystery. Did they both have a darker secret in their lives that had turned them into what they had become? I had been told that my father left Sheffield under a cloud and never returned, not even for the burial of his own parents. He never kept in touch with his brothers. Was he a wild and violent person in his youth? Was there a weakness in his character that he could not contain, that went from bad to worse and broke into an uncontrolled evil under the influence of strong drink?

Mother had children by at least three men. Thirty years later, when she began to talk about her past, the story she told did not ring true. When she ran away from the family to London she started life again, as if her children had never existed, and she never made

144

contact again for twenty-eight years. The day mother walked out of the door of 335 Stonehouse Lane never to return to the house she caught the same number 12 bus that had brought us together as a family from the slums. She was never to be heard of again until she was sixty when she returned as Mrs Palmer and not as Mrs Hicks. She had either changed her name by deed poll or she had married Mr Palmer knowing she was committing bigamy.

My mother left her children to the fear she herself dreaded. She had contributed to the insecurities in Ddad which pushed him over the edge and turned him into a monster when he was under the influence of drink. In mother's life we children counted for nothing and her behaviour brought out the worst elements of Dad's character. Before that final day, mother had already been missing for a few nights but she came back to collect some things. We were totally unaware of mother's plans and thought it was a day like any other. We told her we had had nothing to eat or drink. She said she did not have much money but when she opened her purse I saw some notes. She gave me a few pennies to buy some bread and milk. When I came back from the shop, mother was wearing the check coat, used as an extra blanket during the cold nights. I felt the atmosphere of gloom in the house pressing down on me and my heart sank. No child in a normal

family would miss his mother's coat more than his mother – but I did!

Having seen mother kissing and cuddling Mr Palmer, I knew that she was putting him before us, her own children. Mom was different from other women. She produced children but she did not have a mother's heart. Her body had brought forth seven children but her spirit had not stirred with love and joy or the desire to hold them close to her. Mother was totally absorbed with herself and her own desires. All the hardships of her time and the circumstances of her life had not softened her hard interior.

Any vague hope that mother actually loved us had evaporated since that day at Bellevue and the realisation made me withdraw even more into myself.

Mother wanted her children to hug her – to hug her for the last time. How cruel! Can you imagine the way we felt, being told by our own mother that we must hug her because this would be the last time! I can understand any mother who is dying from

> "I cannot hug you, Mom. I cannot! Cannot! Cannot! I don't want to, because you don't really want to hug me or be near me or understand me. You're always saying you'll leave us and I know you will one day. But it's cold at night and we need your coat on our bed."
>
> — A Child's Thoughts

an incurable disease longing for her children to hug her but to expect and request a farewell gesture at the point of abandoning one's children, seems an unbelievably wicked thing to do. I could not hug her, although eventually she held me to her and I remember the smell, the same smell she'd had when she took me away from the security and care of Erdington Cottage Homes. The same fear that I felt then overcame me. I was more frightened than ever before. The future was bleak. I can remember noticing how calm she was as she went upstairs and collected her belongings. Intuitively I felt that there was something final about her movements but I did not want to acknowledge it.

Mother left on 9 June 1952. It was the year King George VI died and when the *Diary of Anne Frank* was published in English, a heartbreaking story that should have moved any mother's heart. It was the year when Great Britain exploded its first atomic bomb and when America tested its first H-bomb. Our family was living through its own explosive times and the inevitable devastation that followed.

Mother said goodbye to her own flesh and blood, knowing that we would suffer more intensely, over and over again, under the cruel bullying hand of the man she had chosen to marry – a man so violent that she

147

often threatened to get protection from the police. The only reason she had not reported him for vicious treatment of his children was because she wanted to continue her affair with Mr Palmer, a man whose own wife and children were thousands of miles away in the West Indies.

She was hard-hearted enough to look into our little faces, to see the anguish in our eyes, to know our silent and spoken pleas and still say, 'Goodbye'!

As if that were not enough her final insult was to try to transfer the responsibility and guilt for her going, by saying that we had not loved her!

Tens of thousands of women in the war years said tearful and soul-aching goodbyes to their sons, and the separation from their children broke their hearts. Our mother said goodbye to us so that she could live her own selfish life in London. She didn't contact us again until her companion of nearly thirty years died. When she was alone, and looking much older than her years, she came back to us. Maybe we should have told her our true feelings then, but it would have made very little difference to mother.

Stunned, bewildered and confused, the expressions on our sombre faces could only give the faintest hint of the deep feelings swirling like restless ocean waves

A FAMILY ADRIFT

within us. We had been taught at school that animals do not desert their young until they can defend themselves, yet mother was not only deserting us, but telling us she was going.

Part of me did not believe it. Mother had stopped out many times, aggravating Dad and making life even more difficult for us. I wanted to believe that this was just another of those occasions. Yet, deep down, I knew it wasn't.

John realised the gravity of the situation. When the number 12 bus passed our house mother was on it, and it was taking her away! In spite of his asthma, John got on his bike and began to race after the bus. In no time at all his breathing was laboured and his little heart was breaking, but he still thought he could catch up with the big double-decker bus that was taking his mother away into the big unknown world. If he could pedal

fast enough, maybe when the bus halted at the next stop he could jump on it. I do not know whether mother looked back, but it would seem strange to me if she did not. Did she see her suffering son slowly disappear into the distance? John did not catch up with the bus, and he only

> "Why did you say I did not love you, as if it was my fault? Why did you say you were leaving us all, as if it was our fault? Why did you want to say, 'Goodbye'?"
>
> — A Child's Thoughts

saw his mother one more time in his life. A few days after she left, John tracked mother down to where she was living with Mr Palmer. John saw her through the house window and knocked on the door. Mr Palmer swore that she was not there and told John to 'Shove off'. Mother never came to the door to see John. She had already said her final goodbyes.

Jean also left home. She ran away from home, totally disorientated by mother's leaving and full of fear, knowing how Dad would react. As the only girl, she already felt isolated at home. Excluded at home and ridiculed at school, for being poor and having a severe squint in her eyes, her greatest fear had materialised – she was unloved, unwanted, had nowhere to go and didn't know what to do. She roamed the fields as her fears grew and the first night slept under the hedgerows at the bus terminus in Bartley Green.

> "Mom... I don't understand why you have run away and not taken Jean with you!
> Jean is now the only girl, all alone and afraid."
> — A Child's Thoughts

By morning she was very hungry. Without realising it, she was becoming dehydrated and lost within herself – lost in a way that no child should ever feel. She had woken during the night whenever a bus came into the terminus. She saw the bus driver and conductor with mugs of hot tea and packs of

150

sandwiches and imagined that their food and drink had been prepared for them by loving hands. Time and again she was tempted to creep forward to beg for a drink and a bite to eat, but she knew that the next day she would get her free meal at school and after that she would decide what to do.

At five o'clock in the morning she was desperate for a drink, so she went to a nearby house and knocked on the door. The lights in the bedroom came on and a lady opened the door. She could not believe the sight that met her. On her doorstep stood a twelve-year-old girl, looking like death warmed up. Her clothes were filthy, her hair was a mess and her face was tear-stained and dirty. Looking into the girl's misaligned eyes the woman saw fear. Without hesitation she took Jean in and told her husband to call the police. Jean drank cup after cup of water and eventually managed some hot tea and toast.

The policeman arrived on his bike. He soon realised that he would have to take Jean to the regional police station some six miles away, because he wasn't going to be able to persuade Jean to go back home. So, after a restless night, Jean had to walk alongside the policeman as he pushed his bike on their six-mile journey.

Jean refused to go back home. She spent a few days in foster care and succeeded in convincing the local

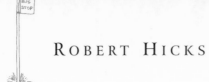

magistrate of her determination not to go back to 335. Contact was made with an uncle and aunt who lived in Sheffield and Jean was eventually transferred there for two years.

At first, she was made welcome. But Dad refused to send them any money for her keep, not even her share of the Family Allowance, so eventually the uncle and aunt falsely accused Jean of being unruly and disrespectful. They said they could no longer look after her.

Of all the children, Jean was faced with the greatest difficulties, not only before Mom left, but also afterwards. She planned to take her own life more than once, and on one occasion nearly succeeded. Of all the children, she has every reason to be proud of herself having overcome such incredible obstacles.

So mother went leaving behind chaos. It was as if until then we had been living next door to Hell but now the door to Hell had been opened wide. The saying 'Hell hath no fury like a woman scorned' applied to Dad. He had been scorned and his fury was of the highest order. Mom had gone on the number 12 bus, and an hour or two later Dad returned home on the same number bus. The moment he walked in, it was obvious he was aggravated as he searched the house for Mom in vain.

152

'Has your Mmom arrived back?'

'Where is she?'

'Where has she gone? What did she take with her?'

'Why did she come back? What did she say?'

'Do you know where she is? Are you hiding something?'

> "John... I am so pleased you are my big brother. I need you. Please don't go away as well."
>
> — A Child's Thoughts

He spat out question after question like bullets from a machine gun. John tried to pacify him. I hardly spoke and only did so when he remembered that I was the one who had called the police once and had spent a day with mother at Bellevue.

In those early days, John saved us from the consequence of Dad's anger and we all pretended that we did not know whether Mom had gone for good. I don't think we convinced Dad and his mood got blacker and his anger hotter.

We were with Dad on his own for a very short time. Soon after Jean went to Sheffield, Bernard and Brian were sent to Shenley Fields Homes. John entered a convalescent home because of his asthma and I went to Middlemore Homes, a huge institution that was used to provide temporary accommodation for homeless children who were emigrating to Canada and Australia.

Middlemore Homes was a huge building

constructed with money from the Cadbury brothers who established their confectionery company in Birmingham. They generously donated funds to benefit working-class people and Birmingham's cultural life. They moved their premises from the city centre to a site ten miles south of Birmingham, where they built their huge chocolate factories and a superb modern village to house their workers. The houses were built to a high standard, giving light and air and open spaces. They set new standards. If local councils and business organisations had followed their pattern, the social framework of our cities would have been vastly improved. They contributed to the huge Birmingham Library as well as the Art Gallery, ensuring that such masterpieces as the Pre-Raphaelites would be preserved. In time, their generosity was recognised worldwide. The Cadburys were always concerned about minority groups who were marginalised in society and they provided funding for the Westhill Teacher Training College which is now part of Birmingham University. Middlemore Homes stood across the road from Westhill College. It was an institution for waifs and strays, whether orphaned or ill-treated at home, and up to 1948 was used as a temporary centre for those unfortunate children who would eventually leave these Islands and go to

154

work on the farms of Australia and Canada. The staff at the Homes made every effort to ensure there was a good match between the children and the families abroad, but inevitably there were some failures.

Aunt Lily, mother's younger sister, was going to take me to the Homes. I was told she would call for me in the morning and that I would get something to eat once I'd arrived. She came late in the afternoon and made it clear she was not happy at being required to make such a long journey when Dad should have done it himself. The journey to Middlemore Homes took two buses and a long walk. I remember the walk, which led past a vast burial ground surrounded by a brick wall. I wanted to know what was on the other side of the wall and when we came to the main gates I looked through and saw rows and rows of graves. I think that was the first time I realised that a lot of people had died. I knew that people had died in the war, but seeing all those old gravestones impressed on me the reality of death in a very dramatic way.

Middlemore Homes was huge. The buildings were arranged as three sides of a square. Two wings were linked together by an amazing building with a large portico over the central doors. We didn't go in through the central doors but by a side entrance. A junior assistant led us down a long corridor. We passed through large doors into a central hallway where there

> "Today I only got dry sandwiches. I was expecting hot food like I got at the other Children's Home.
> I hoped that nice cuddly lady would be here with her smiling face but it's a different Home.
> How I miss her!"
>
> — A Child's Thoughts

were rows and rows of tables with children sitting round them playing *Housey Housey* before they went to bed. The winner got a boiled sweet! The man stopped calling out numbers and came over to Aunt Lily. Within moments Aunt Lily left, telling me to behave myself or my Dad would find out. I thought she might give me a few pennies or sweets before leaving me, but she didn't. Perhaps she too was finding life difficult.

Middlemore Homes was huge. I felt very small as I sat at a table in this massive central hall. There were some curled-up sandwiches, a glass of milk and a slice of angel cake. The man went back to finish the game, while I was left to consume the sandwiches. I was so hungry that I ate those sandwiches like a wolf even though they were dry and had stale crusts. I was still extremely hungry after I'd finished but the only consolation I received was to be given one of the boiled sweets. The man in charge made it clear this was an extra, and I should not expect one every night unless I won *Housey Housey*.

After a short time, a younger man, Mr Swift, came in. His duty had been extended to prepare me for bed. He kept looking at his watch, because he had a date with a young lady and wanted to go. The other boys had already gone to their dormitories. I had to have a hair cut and a shower. Mr Swift told me to take my clothes off. He wouldn't touch them. They were put into a plastic bag, never to be seen again! Nothing that I wore that day was kept.

He cut my hair with sharp scissors, leaving me with short spikey hair that reminded me of a hedgehog. I was not aware of having headlice, although it was possible. I stood under a cold shower which gradually became lukewarm. A large dollop of black disinfectant was poured on my head and rubbed into my scalp. It ran down my body like black tram lines. This was the first time that I was aware of being naked in front of anybody and I was embarrassed. Mr Swift's girlfriend had arrived too, and though she had a happy, welcoming, understanding smile on her lips, her presence only added to my embarrassment.

After I'd showered, Mr Swift gave me a pair of pyjamas which were far too long. He told me to roll up the sleeves and legs. Finally we made what seemed like an endless journey up to the

157

dormitory. It was a huge room full of army beds, like a hospital ward. There were twenty-five beds in all, twelve on one side and thirteen on the other. The lights had been out, but they were put back on for me to see my way to the end of the room. As I walked past the beds I saw the boys lifting their heads off their pillows to get a look at the new boy. I felt I was gate-crashing their world and that I would never belong there.

My bed was the last but one on the right, not too far from a fire exit door. The last bed was empty. The other boys said the bed had been left vacant ever since the last boy who slept there had tried to escape through the fire exit and had fallen and killed himself. I think they had over-dramatised a previous incident but it left a vivid impression on my mind. I was tired and hungry, but I felt better for the shower, disinfectant and clean pyjamas. When I climbed up into the high army bed I slid between clean sheets! They were white and starched with real creases in them. There was a pillow inside a pillowcase and the bed was mine alone. I did not have to share it with anybody.

Nothing prepared me for the huge barrack-style

institutions which eventually gave way to the more humane fostering where children could join real families and enjoy personal attention. The smell of these institutions was so different to the slums and to the countryside. Disinfectant was used in such generous quantities that I did not want to breathe in too deeply. I was no different to the other children, but the very size of the buildings made me apprehensive and fearful. I did not know who I was, what I could do, why I was there, how long I would be there or where I would go afterwards. If I felt a stranger as I so often did, in my own family, then I felt much more lost and abandoned in these vast buildings. The dormitory, with its highly polished wooden floor was for sleeping in only. The main room where we had our meals could easily seat two hundred, although there were only about fifty of us, which made me feel very conspicuous.

Adjacent to the institution was a small concrete playground. Indoors the only game we were allowed to play was *Housey Housey* and everyone had to participate in it. Every morning and evening we had a shower. It made me think how dirty I was when I lived at home

> "My Mom has gone.
> My hair has gone.
> My clothes have gone.
> My family has gone.
> I am all alone again."
>
> — A Child's Thoughts

159

where there was no such luxury as a shower. Emotionally, I always felt I was a nobody at the institution. I was lost among the other boys, and the staff seemed to think I needed to be regimented in order to maintain discipline and control.

> "I am still hungry, but now I feel clean inside and out after the shower and now this bed that smells so nice.
> I wonder what will happen next."
>
> — A Child's Thoughts

During my time in institutional care, there was only one lady who showed me genuine loving affection which came from the heart. Although my encounter with that lady was brief, it taught me that human love is the most powerful natural influence in the world for good. Children especially need that human dimension for it can perform a miracle, as it did with me. It prevented me from growing up cynical, negative and even aggressive towards a system that devalues rather than elevates the dignity of the individual.

I was eleven years of age and traumatised once again. I had been taken away from the countryside I loved and put in an Middlemore Homes. I recalled some of the good things I'd experienced when I had been put in an institution – clean sheets, hot food, security, freedom from arguments, fights and beatings. Maybe it would not be so bad being in Middlemore

Homes. But I couldn't shake off the darker mood which overcame me. I was deserted. I was separated from my brothers and sister. I was unloved and unwanted. Deep down I felt useless and unwelcome. Although I was the loner, I missed my brothers and sister. This emptiness was a constant ache inside me.

I was tired that first night but I didn't go to sleep until I'd visualised again my little robin fighting with all his might against being trapped in a cage. In the morning, the children got ready for school. First I had to be rigged out with clothes. We all wore grey clothes, which marked us out as children whose parents or families were not providing for us. To my amazement, I was sent back to the school that I attended when I lived at 335. Ilmington Secondary Modern School segregated the boys from the girls. It lay mid-way between Bartley Green and Middlemore Homes at Selly Oak so I was still able to walk to school.

For the first time, I set off for school well-dressed, wearing shoes that did not have holes in the soles. I had a vest and pants on under my shirt and trousers and it felt strange to wear so many clothes. I went to school feeling quite proud of being so smart, but by the time I returned I'd had that sense of pride ridiculed out of me. The other lower-class children took the mickey out of me for having been placed in an institution. Even those classed as the poorest of the poor still had their parents. I was further down the scale than them. I had reached the bottom of the pit. The boys at school must have thought I deserved it, and their taunts penetrated me like arrows.

After being in the institution for a few days, a boy called Billy approached me. He was smaller than me and had some other boys with him. He rolled up his sleeves, put his fists together like a boxer and challenged me to fight to see who would be Cock of the Home. It was obvious that he was used to throwing his weight around and was determined that a new boy was not going to take his place.

I was used to pain and Dad had regularly done shadow boxing with us to toughen us up, as he used to say, but I had never been involved in a serious fight and didn't want to be. Enunciating as clearly as I could, I told the boy that if he wanted me to fight then I would but I would prefer to be his friend. I can see his face now. Someone offering to be his friend left him

> "I look strange in the grey clothes and they feel so heavy, but I know they are not really mine. Children at school also know they don't belong to me and they make fun of me."
>
> — A Child's Thoughts

confused. He smiled and dropped his hands to his sides. Then he stuck out a hand of welcome and we shook and became friends. I learnt a very important lesson: that children in deprived circumstances desperately need a friend, no matter what their outward behaviour suggests. That simple text on the wall at 335, about the 'Perfect Friend', often came to mind.

Billy told one of the staff that I was a very good footballer. We had played one or two games of football on a concrete pavement at the Homes, but I had never been in a real game on a pitch. However, he got me into the football team and the following week I played in defence. The member of staff in charge was pleased because I was able to kick the ball fast and hard, sending it deep into the opposition's half. My reputation as a good defender was made!

163

When I looked at the other children around me I felt sorry for them. Some were orphaned, the parents of others had divorced and some had simply been abandoned. Many of the boys were thin and weak, whereas in our family all of us, except for Bernard, were sturdily built, which was just as well considering the kind of life we had lived at home.

Although I felt unable to express my feelings perhaps some of the boys became aware of my sympathy for them because soon they gravitated towards me. I wondered if Billy, the 'Cock of the Home' would become jealous but we had become friends and he did not appear to feel threatened by me.

No one at the institution or at school did anything about my being tongue-tied. I had learnt to make sounds using the muscles in the back of my throat and tongue, so my problem with enunciation was simply assumed to be lazy speech.

One morning, after about six months in Middlemore Homes, one of the staff told me to go to school as usual but not to return to the institution. Instead I was to go back to my father and meet up with my brothers. I am not aware of anyone taking me back to 335 but I can remember them taking all the grey clothes from me and fitting me out with a combination of second-hand ones. They were far superior to the rags I had arrived in, but they did not fit as well or feel as good as the grey clothes.

To go back to Stonehouse Lane at the end of the school day seemed strange. Perhaps Dad had changed but I did not really think so. I didn't know what to do.

I was nearly twelve when I left the institution. Although I had mixed feelings about the place, I was loathe to give up the security I had gained there: I had been the centre of a small group; I had played in the football team; I had been commended for defending.

Back at 335 Dad seldom stayed in when we were at home. We became dependent on the free meals at school again. We soon reverted to running wild, although we did have to keep the house clean. John became the buffer between Dad and the rest of us and he organised us. On one occasion he took us to play cricket in the nearby park with some other boys. I observed how he swung the bat and hit the ball. Several girls gathered around us and John was very disappointed when I ran towards a gap and, remarkably for me, caught and held on to the ball. He was out! Soon it was my turn to bat. Just as I had been a defender on the football pitch, so that day I seemed to defend the wicket endlessly and made many runs. John was getting frustrated and suggested I should declare. The idea of declaring and becoming a mid-fielder did not appeal to me. I was in for so long that the others got weary and

> "Today, I made friends with the leader of a 'gang'. He needs a friend. All the boys need a friend. Inside they are so empty."
> — A Child's Thoughts

> "I watched a spider making its web in the bushes. Although it spends a long time making its web, I know that tomorrow it will have lots of breaks in it and the spider will start all over again. The teacher keeps telling me to try and try again to read. I do keep trying, but I can't see the words on the page. I really do want to learn to read and, like the spider, I don't mind trying again... but I just can't see the words on the page. How can other children see the words to read?"
>
> — A Child's Thoughts

gave up on the game.

During this time with Dad we began to act out two parallel lives. We did not talk about what went on in our house behind closed doors. Maybe we were too ashamed to do so but what happened outside was an antidote to all the bullying and ritual interrogations which took place inside. I got a sick feeling in the pit of my stomach every time I was called down to that narrow cold kitchen to be tormented by Dad. His behaviour became worse because of the amount of alcohol he drank. He was a bully and for years I tried to pacify him. If I was the only child at home I made sure the place was clean, the lino polished, the cast-iron black fireplace spotless and shining and the surfaces dusted. I didn't eat all the bread and wouldn't touch his bacon. I would starve rather than give Dad any excuse

to go berserk. I often wondered whether his mind had been affected by what he witnessed in the concentration camps in Germany, but I realised the root of the problem was much closer to home. It was all to do with mother leaving.

That text on the wall at 335 about the 'Perfect Friend' who knows the best and worst about us and loves us just the same, both encouraged and distressed me. Deep down, I knew there must be a friend somewhere out there, and I so badly needed a friend. But even as I thought about my own need, I knew that I also wanted to be a friend to others, even though I could never be a perfect one. I longed to give and receive acceptance. I longed for friendship. The simple ideas behind that text slowly brought comfort and renewal to my crushed spirit and I needed its moral and spiritual strength to help me face the uncertain future.

CHAPTER 7
335 WITHOUT MOM

CHAPTER 7

335 WITHOUT MOM

All around me was a living countryside that had taken a thousand years to shape into the landscape I experienced and loved but in those early teenage years I just felt lost.

I was alone with no sense of purpose. I was unable to take any advice from anyone. I had become suspicious and nobody loved me, just for being me.

A specialist with knowledge of dyslexia would have rewired my brain so that my thoughts were no longer be trapped in my head! A surgeon would have understood the torment of having

"It's blue. It's green.
It's brown. It's silver.
It's bright. It's dark.
It's lots of colours.

I love it. I see it.
I smell it.
It's all around me.

I am part of it.
I am full of it;
every part of me.

It keeps changing.
No two days are the
same.

And it's free!
And it's mine
when I'm away
from home."

— A Child's Thoughts

an intelligence that was growing, observing, discerning, understanding, but could not express itself, so that the exterior that other people saw resembled an idiot, a fool, a stupid person who should be pitied.

A schoolteacher would have seen that I needed speech therapy and help with reading and writing and would have had the time, the patience, and the finance to help me a youngster dressed in charity clothes.

I was lost, and all alone, and I felt it deeply.

Walking along the riverbanks I picked up stones and threw them into the water. Just as those stones disappeared beneath the surface, I felt my life was sinking into oblivion.

I grasped every distraction I could find to escape for a moment from that sense of being powerless to alter who I was, where I was from and where I was going.

I was lost and all alone and there were no parents, no doctors, no teachers who could see the potential within me that was worth rescuing. I cried, but no one heard the cries, because they were silent! The sound was trapped deep, deep inside me. In the trailer to the film, *Alien* the voice-over said: 'What's the use of screaming out loud into deep space, when no one is there?' I knew precisely what the film-makers were trying to convey.

There was little money for the basics at home for

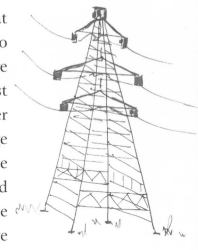

Dad like mother was hopeless at managing money. They spent too much at the local pub and picture house and Dad wouldn't change just because Mom had gone. Mother used to run up a slate at the village shop across the road from our house which would be paid off when Dad got his wages at the weekend. He too would run up debts while we went hungry.

I tried to keep out of the house and out of Dad's way but sometimes that got me into trouble. There were giant electrical pylons in the park at Bartley Green. Part way up the pylons was a barrier of wire to prevent anyone climbing them. We used to climb as far as the wire but no further although there were steps to the top.

Once I was given a double dare to climb to the top. In spite of my fear of heights, and probably because I wanted to impress the other children, I negotiated the wire protection and eventually climbed to the top. I didn't look down so I didn't realise how high I was. When I reached the top and heard the whirring noise of the cables, I became very afraid. I looked down and my head started spinning. The other children were shouting to me to come down but all I could do was to

173

lean against the pylon and wait for the giddiness to subside. Then, from a distance, I saw the park keeper running towards the pylon. I knew if he caught me he would take me to Dad and that frightened me more than being on the top of the pylon. I descended so quickly that I was able to make my escape before the park-keeper reached me. He asked the children where I lived. That evening, he appeared at the house and told my father. Fortunately for me, Dad was on his way out, his trousers and shirt neatly ironed, his silk scarf wrapped around his neck and his silver-plated cigarette holder in his pocket. He told me he would deal with me when he got back and that I must not go out. As soon as he left I went out roaming, but I made sure I was back early and in bed before Dad came home.

> "I know inside my heart I cry a lot. But no-one can see the tears. I even cry inside when I am smiling outside. I don't want them to know I have been crying. When I grow up, I will never cry again because when I am an adult no-one will be able to hurt me."
>
> — A Child's Thoughts

174

When we were in bed, we always made sure we put a peg in the door lock to make it difficult for Dad to get in. We would pretend to be asleep and refused to answer when he called because we knew what would happen. This tactic often worked and undoubtedly saved us from many a beating. Incredibly, Dad never did deal with me over the pylon incident and never talked about it again. Somehow things like that did not bother him. All his interrogations and accusations were related to Mom, not to the way we children were behaving. He seemed oblivious to our need of parenting.

Another memorable incident was when Bernard, Brian and I were playing with some other boys by a large oak tree alongside a wide stream. A branch hung over the stream and there was a long rope tied to it. An easy game involved swinging out over the stream and landing safely back on the same bank. A more dangerous game was to swing out over the stream, allow the rope to slow down, climb up it, go along the branch and climb down the tree. I was able to climb ropes so it wasn't difficult but Brian, who was always willing to take risks, tried it even though he couldn't swim. He landed in the water and would have drowned if some of the bigger boys hadn't fished him out.

When I had a few pennies I usually spent them on going to the cinema. One day I was on my way to an early evening film at the Weoley Castle Picture House. I arrived to see a mad dog attacking two girls who went

to my school. I plucked up courage and tried to subdue the dog. I told the doorman at the picture house to let the girls inside. At first he refused but I told him I would push the mad dog inside if he did not let the girls in. He ushered them in immediately. I wound my mackintosh around my arm and went towards the dog. It watched my every move. Its eyes were wild and flashing and it was foaming at the mouth. Suddenly the animal flung itself at me and sank its teeth into my arm and locked its jaws. I began to swing round and round. Slowly the mac unwound until I was just holding the end of it. The dog held on grimly. I increased my speed, although I was getting dizzy and my arm was aching. When I let go of the mac both it and the dog flew through the air and the poor mad creature smashed into a tree trunk. For a moment I thought it was dead, but then it showed signs of life. I had lost my mac which was my only protection. I needed to get inside the picture house before the dog attacked me again. A car sped towards the cinema. When the dog heard the roar of the engine, it ran straight at the car and was run over. I retrieved my mac and walked away feeling ten feet tall! Before long the story was going round at school that Bobby Hicks had killed a mad dog just like Samson had killed a lion. I was, for a time, the centre of attention and even I began to believe I had exceptional strength.

One day my strength was put to the test. A gypsy used to come to the Bull Ring market area in Birmingham city centre and earn pennies off the shoppers by tearing telephone books in half. I watched him carefully and saw how he was doing it, then I called out from the crowd that I could do the same. He promptly gave me a book and I managed to copy his act. I thought he would have been deflated, but instead he used the occasion to extract more pennies from his onlookers and refused to share his financial bonus with me!

> "The world is spinning round fast according to the teacher at school. I have worked out that if I jump high enough, the earth will spin beneath me and I will land in a place further on. Maybe I have found a new way of travelling! The women who live nearby look at me strangely while I test my new idea."
>
> — A Child's Thoughts

177

Not all my efforts were successful. There was a part of a stream that none of us were able to jump across. I wanted to do it and decided to try. Two people were walking towards me and I waited until they got nearer so they would see me succeed. I flung myself through the air but I had not gauged the distance properly. I hit the opposite bank and slipped back into the water up to my knees. The woman called out to enquire whether

ROBERT HICKS

I was all right, which embarrassed me all the more. I scrambled out of the water, muttered 'Yes', waved to them and walked away feeling very foolish for having made such a spectacle of myself.

Several new families had moved into the recently built houses in my lane. The Keys lived on the same side as us but further down the road. Mr Keys was a small, hard-working man and the family seemed happy, although the children were somewhat wild like us. Mickey Keys only had one eye. He told me he lost his other eye when he fell out of the big oak tree on the verge in front of their house. I discovered the truth many years later. Mickey lost his eye when he and his brother were playing with a catapult and stones. It was a secret and his parents went to their graves not knowing what really happened.

I had not been back at home long when two of the Keys girls invited me into their house. They said their Mom and Dad had gone out for the evening. At first we played downstairs then the two girls ran upstairs and told me to follow them in a few moments. As I went upstairs they came out of their mother's bedroom, each wrapped only in a towel. They had powdered their faces and slapped on some of their mother's lipstick. I was shocked to the core. Then they purposely dropped their towels and went into fits of giggles at the expression on my face. I felt myself

178

blushing to the roots of my hair which made them laugh even more. At that point I heard Mr Keys shouting up the stairs. Their plans for an evening out hadn't materialised so they had come home. They were surprised to find me upstairs and told me in no uncertain terms that upstairs was out of bounds. I left as quickly as I could. I have no idea what Mr and Mrs Keys said to their girls but I found it very difficult to look them in the eye for a long time. Nevertheless, Mrs Keys was always happy to see us and give us a drink of juice. Later, I learnt that she was not married to Mr Keys. When Mr Keys' wife had died, she became his housekeeper. She had already been married two or three times, and she moved in with her children. They lived together as man and wife, something unheard of in those days. She was a kind, warm, happy woman and the family was lovely.

179

An older couple lived in another of the new houses with their daughter, son-in-law and grandson. They always dressed nicely and were posh compared to the rest of us. I was invited in once. The house was decorated and furnished in a modern style but what stuck in my memory more than the décor was the drink she gave me. She asked if I would like a fizzy

drink and when I said I would she put a spoonful of Andrew's Liver Salts in some warm water, stirred it and told me to drink it immediately. It was the most peculiar drink I had ever tasted! One Christmas the grandson was given a new cricket set which included two bats. In the spring we commandeered it and organised a match. He was out after the first few balls and went home to complain to his mother who came and took the cricket set from us.

I got to know most of our neighbours because I was always happy to do errands for them, not least because it could result in a piece of cake or a drink, and sometimes a few pennies which I could save up to visit the picture house. On one occasion, Mrs Philpott from the village shop sent me on an errand to the post office to get a fifteen shilling postal order. This meant a journey to the top of Jiggins Lane so she gave me the bus fare but said she didn't mind if I wanted to walk and keep the money for myself. I walked to save the bus fare and finally reached the post office. A young girl served me. I asked for a fifteen shilling postal order and handed her a pound note. By accident she gave me fifteen shillings change instead of five. I did not realise she had made a mistake at first but on my way home I stopped to check the postal order and discovered I had a fifteen shilling postal order and fifteen shillings in change! I did not know what to do. Should I take the postal order to Mrs Philpott first or should I return the overpaid ten shillings straight away? I decided to go to Mrs Philpott but I didn't tell her what had happened. Mrs Philpott gave me sixpence for my effort. I started back towards the post office, but as I jogged along I became more and more tempted to keep the extra money. With ten shillings I could go to the pictures many times and have a bag of chips on the way home. It would be my secret! Ten shillings was a fortune, far more than I had ever owned. I slowed to a walk. By the time I was half way up Jiggins Lane, l had decided to keep the money. It weighed heavily on my conscience. I wondered whether the girl who had served me would have to pay back the ten shillings herself. I did not go anywhere near the post office for a long time and each time I saw Mrs Philpott I half expected her to ask, 'Bobby, what happened to the other ten shillings?'

One evening I went to a film starring Henry Fonda

> "Today I kept ten shillings that was not mine.
> I feel ashamed. Ten shillings is the most money I have ever had.
> I spent a few pennies and I really did want to take the rest back, but I knew I would be in trouble for spending the pennies.
> It was not worth having that money that did not belong to me. It worried me too much. I don't want to get bad like Dad."
>
> — A Child's Thoughts

181

called, *Ten Angry Men*. The film was set in a courtroom
and most of the action took place in a side room where
the jury gathered to discuss the case. A boy was on
trial for killing his father in an act of rage, after his
father had violently assaulted his mother. I could
identify with many aspects of the film yet, what
really bothered me was the guilt of keeping the ten
shillings.

A few weeks later Mrs Philpott asked
me to run another errand to the post office.

I was in a quandary. I did not want to go for
fear of being found out! The same girl was at the
counter and she recognised me. She enquired whether
by accident I had received ten shillings too much the
previous week. I lied and gave her an innocent, hurt
look. She brushed it aside saying that it must have
been someone else. Although I was never brought to
book over the stealing or the lying, both weighed
heavily on my mind, which proves that, even though
the home environment may not be contributing to a
moral or spiritual life, one's conscience still works!

On the way home from school we sometimes used
to pinch a bottle of milk if there were three or four
bottles on a doorstep. Once I went to take a bottle of
milk and noticed a bag of clothes on the step. I took
that too but soon discovered that it contained ladies
clothes from the dry-cleaners! They were of no use at

all to me, so I dumped them. Again, I felt very guilty. I had stolen something that I didn't even need. Although my sister used to regularly shoplift an apple or pear from the greengrocer because she was so hungry. I only ever stole from a shop once. It was a sweet shop in Weoley Castle, not far from the senior school. The shopkeeper had a club foot. At lunchtime the shop was packed with children buying liquorice, gobstoppers, aniseed balls, pear drops, and other sweets. I had no money, but used to go in hoping that I might be able to steal a bar of chocolate. I had never eaten a bar of chocolate, but I still remembered my bar of Cadbury's that Donald shared

> "Will I ever have some chocolate again? It is such a long time since Donald stole my bar of chocolate. I wonder how much longer I will have to wait."
> — A Child's Thoughts

183

with John when I was six. I kept going into the shop trying to pluck up courage, but I could not do so. Then one day, when the shopkeeper was serving another child, I reached out to take a bar of chocolate. In an instant he brought his walking stick down across my hand and told me that as I had no intention of buying anything, to leave the shop. He never knew how sorry I was for my behaviour and for his disability because I said nothing and I never went into the shop again.

Toffee apples were popular at school lunchtimes.

An enterprising grandmother started making toffee apples and sold them for a halfpenny each if they were small or a penny each for large ones. She sold two or three dozen every day. The first time I was able to afford one I really enjoyed it. I began to collect empty drinks bottles which had been thrown away but could be sold back to the shopkeeper. This way I made enough money to treat myself. I couldn't afford a toffee apple every week but I was able to buy one regularly. I seldom shared my toffee apple, although I was expected to give the apple core to anyone more needy than me! I had been glad to accept cores in the past, so I willingly gave mine away.

> "A lady who lives near school sells toffee apples at lunch break time.
> I sometimes get the 'core' from other children and sometimes there's a bit of toffee apple left too.
> I like toffee apple. I am going to save some pennies to buy one all to myself. One day I will have a toffee apple all to myself."
>
> — A Child's Thoughts

Back at home there were brief periods of calm but there was not a single moment of the joy there. Then Brian ran away. He had stopped out all night on many occasions, but this time days had elapsed and he had not returned. Finally, dad called the police. They searched the area extensively without success. The army was called in to assist them.

He was found a few days later, just a few miles away. He had been living off vegetables stolen from allotments and sheltered wherever he could. Brian was sent to a boys' institution in Handsworth. He was now marked as a bad boy even though he wasn't.

Bernard's asthma had worsened, perhaps because of the stress of not having mother at home. He was sent to Blackwell Convalescent Home. There was an open school nearby. It was a very sad time for Bernard. He received little schooling and spent most of his time walking alone in the open air or sleeping in an army bed next to a window which stayed open regardless of the weather. Bernard not only felt isolated from his family but unwanted too. Nobody visited him and this was especially painful because all the other children received regular visitors.

John also spent periods away convalescing, but even when he was at home, he seemed more absent and invisible than ever before. He was no longer there to pacify Dad as he had been in the past.

Dad's late night interrogations continued. Sometimes it was on the odd occasion during the week and sometimes it seemed to be every night. The constant allegations, the questioning, the bullying and

the violence wore me down. I cried. I cried a thousand times but no tears were visible. I had few successes at school, other than in maths. I had some talent as a sprinter but there was no coaching system in place to encourage me and develop my potential. I could have been in the football team but I played truant too often! I was frequently caned for arriving late at school. Usually it was because I had to go to buy Dad's newspaper before I could start on my journey to school. Whenever I told Dad that it made me late for school he didn't want to know.

Now that Dad and I were the only one living at 335 I had to clean the house and do all the cooking and washing. Despite all I did in the house Dad never thanked me, and never said that I had done a good job. Instead, he found fault with everything. Once I reached my teens, I would scrape together a few pennies and escape into the fantasy world of the pictures to get away from life at home.

> "I am all alone with Dad and I don't know what I have done to deserve this."
> — A Child's Thoughts

A lady called at the house regularly selling items from a catalogue and Dad occasionally bought something from her. Once I saw some clothes in the catalogue that I liked, including a pair of long trousers. When she came round the next time, she saw that I was interested and suggested that I got a paper-round or a milk-round and earned some money to purchase the clothes.

A week later she came to collect the catalogue and told me there was a milk-round available with her milkman. The milkman was a tall man in his twenties. He had a very happy disposition and was always telling jokes. The rude ones were wasted on me! I soon learnt how to carry three bottles in each hand as I ran up and down paths, leaving the full bottles and bringing back the empties. The empties were as important to the milkman as the full ones and he constantly complained about the empty bottles that went missing.

One cold morning we stopped at Rosie's Cafe. It was not far from where I lived although I had never been inside. The people in the cafe knew the milkman well. A very large, jolly lady with a broad, happy face and a laugh that went with it stood behind the counter. After she had served us with a mug of tea she asked me if I wanted a tomato dip. I had no money for one and I did not think the milkman would want to buy one for me, but she said I could have it on the house. I had never eaten a tomato dip before. It was a thick slice of bread dipped in the white of an egg and smothered in tinned tomatoes. It was piping hot and absolutely delicious! The only other time I had enjoyed a similar

187

> "I had a cup of coffee today in a china cup with Mrs. Taylor and a digestive biscuit. I have never tasted anything so nice before! This is the first time I have ever had a whole biscuit.
> I never knew that drinking from a proper cup and saucer could make a drink taste so nice. I wish we had cups and saucers and whole biscuits."
>
> — A Child's Thoughts

sensation was when Mrs Taylor gave me a whole digestive biscuit to eat with a cup of milky coffee. I thought I had never tasted anything as nice in my life.

One day the milkman drove round to a large house in a road I didn't know. He spoke to the lady at the door. I was surprised that she was still in her nightdress as it was late. After a few moments he went inside. She called me to the door, gave me some money and told me to go and get her a loaf of bread. She said I should take my time and go to the shop furthest down the road as the first one did not sell bread. I ran to the first shop and could see through the window that it stocked bread. So I bought a loaf and got back to the house much more quickly than anticipated. I rang the bell and after what seemed a long time she answered the door. She seemed flustered and told me to go and look at the rabbit in a cage in the garden. There were a pair of rabbits in the cage and a litter of babies. It was a long time before I realised that it was not only the rabbits doing what rabbits do on that day. When the milkman finally came out of the big house, we returned to the depot to pay in his takings. He was £2 short. The blood drained from his face and he begged me to tell him I'd taken it. He was desperate, but I hadn't taken the money. Whatever had happened at the big house, he had paid dearly for it. The following week he invited me to his home. I met his wife who had just had her second child. They were living in a new council house. Everything was modern and they seemed very happy. I hoped the fright he suffered when he lost the money served as a warning to him to steer well clear of anything that would damage his family.

Each week I gave all the money I'd earned to the catalogue lady until one Saturday morning Dad insisted that I gave the money to him. He said that I ought to be paying him something towards the cost of my keep. I pleaded with him to let me have the money for clothes but, as I tried to reason with him, Dad's mood changed. He ordered me to go and get the money. I made my way to the lady's house and for the first time I can remember, I cried. I told her what had happened and she was very sympathetic but said I had

to obey my father and she gave me the money which came to just over ten shillings.

With this large amount of money in my pocket, I decided I was not going home. I would try and find work somewhere else and become a successful businessman! I took a bus to the centre of Birmingham. This was an experience in itself. The only time I could remember being in Birmingham was Christmas 1946. It was busy. The streets were snarled up with traffic. When I reached the bus station I realised that I could not read the destinations. I found one which started with the word 'red', a familiar word, so I decided to jump on that bus. The bus was going to Redditch. The fare was ninepence and although the journey took over an hour, Redditch was not that far from home.

An elderly woman was sitting on the other side of the bus. After we had gone a few stops she came over, offered me an apple and asked if I was alright. I thanked her for the apple and said I was fine. I spent the day walking round getting hungrier and hungrier. I ended up in a cafe where they served breakfast all day. Although it was mid-afternoon I enjoyed the most marvellous meal of bacon, eggs, sausages, tomatoes, mushrooms, beans and fried bread, followed by toast and marmalade and a cup of sweet tea. I never had food like this at home! I wandered further out of

Redditch into the countryside. I spent that
night in a wheat field unable to sleep
because of the unfamiliar sounds and my
dread of creepy-crawlies. It was very cold.
At first I lay on my mac, but I was so cold
I had to lie on the earth and wrap the mac
round me. I hardly slept, but I worked out
a plan. I would get work on one of the
farms and when I was older the daughter of the
household would marry me and my future would be
secure!

What actually happened was that around five or six
in the morning a policeman cycled by on his way to
report for duty. He saw me and stopped to question
me. I told him that I had an appointment to work on
the farm but he saw through my story and took me
with him to the police station. I was given a hot cup of
tea and a bacon sandwich and spent the rest of the
morning in a cell catching up on my sleep. A few hours
later, I was put back on the bus home. The conductor
was told to put me off at Selly Oak where I had to
report at the police station. In those days we always did
what the police told us to do. Selly Oak police station
was frantically busy. I felt intimidated and certain that
I was wasting police time. After a long wait, a
policeman accompanied me to 335 Stonehouse Lane.
It was a five-mile walk. He told Dad not to punish me

ROBERT HICKS

as I had been in a cell and had promised not to run away from home again. As soon as the policeman left, Dad smacked me hard across the ear, but that was all and he never referred to my running away again.

One improvement at home was Dad's acquisition of a wireless. We enjoyed listening to *The Archers* a daily serial story about country folk. With all the farms around Bartley Green being sold off and the land being used for new council housing, I wondered how long programmes like *The Archers* would pull in the listeners. One of the disadvantages of owning a wireless that ran on valves and acid batteries was the chore of getting the batteries recharged when they ran down. We had to take them to a special shop in Harborne and since batteries could not be transported by bus, two of us had to carry them in a bag each holding a handle. On one occasion, we did chance it on the bus back from Harborne but we were found out and the

> "Dad wanted my milk-round money that I had saved up. That's not fair. It's my money.
> So I ran away with it to Redditch.
> The policeman picked me up the next morning and sent me back to Selly Oak Police Station. They took me back to Dad.
> There is nowhere to go but back to Dad.
> I am very sad indeed.
> I have no way of getting away."
>
> — A Child's Thoughts

192

conductor put us off the bus. At least we had got a free lift part way because the conductor didn't charge us! Those were the days when bus conductors took their job very personally and regarded the bus as theirs, rather than the bus company's property.

The wireless brought news of the outside world into our home. It was 1953 and I was twelve years of age. There was a general feeling of optimism in the west. The coronation of the young Queen Elizabeth, who touched the hearts of her subjects throughout the Commonwealth and beyond, was attended by most of the world leaders. Hollywood produced the first wide-screen film which was two and a half times as wide as it was high. The film was *The Robe* starring Richard Burton and it captured people's imagination. Rocky Marciano was once again the world heavyweight boxing champion. Gandhi's dream for a united India had been shattered because of the religious divide between the Hindus and the Muslims. The Empires of Great Britain and France were gradually breaking up and smaller imperial powers followed suit. Israel had become an independent state. A new description for the poorer nations was coined 'The Third World', and the term was used regularly in the news. A new aeroplane, the Boeing 747, was tested

and the first pocket-sized transistor radio came on to the market. In Michigan, Detroit's new shopping experience opened. It was called a mall and was an enclosed air-conditioned environment containing up to three hundred shops in arcades on several levels, with a wide range of facilities such as child care, restaurants and free car parking. This new type of shopping brought hope for the revival of many cities that had been run down since the war years. We heard about the tragic floods in the east of England in which nearly three hundred people died but we heard joyful news too – the reports of the coronation and John Hunt's expedition to Everest. The world was changing but the latter two events gave the nation a genuine moral boost.

On the day of the coronation, Mr Philpott organised a street party for the children. Everyone was expected to contribute to the cost but Dad gave nothing. People said we were going to have the best party of the century. A huge bonfire was going to be lit outside our house. This made me particularly proud because it was the Hicks family who had started the tradition of having a bonfire outside 335 on Guy Fawkes night. The men in the street brought massive logs of wood and started building the bonfire. Mr Philpott filled his wagon with wood and piled it on. The boys who lived in the lane added timber they had acquired and before long people were putting on old settees and chairs. Sometimes the furniture was there one day and missing the next! We had to protect our bonfire from raids, to prevent other people stealing our wood for their fire. Competition was in the air but our bonfire was going to be the biggest around! A few years later the police stopped us building our bonfires because they were too high and dangerous.

The local council decorated a number 12 bus in celebration of the coronation. We were captivated by its brilliant fairy lights as it passed along our road with music blaring forth from inside. Many years later I saw an advertisement for Coca Cola with a train and many coaches decked out with yellow lights, but there was nothing quite like the lights on that number 12 bus.

195

There was an incredible atmosphere on Coronation Day itself. People I had not seen for years came out of their houses! The children wore party hats and sat down to a meal of sandwiches, jelly, cake and biscuits. Every child received a present but because Dad had not contributed to the funds we were not included. We did not get a present or a party hat but we did share the food and the drink! There were games, some of which we joined in, and a fancy dress parade. Feeling a little bit cheeky, I put my name down to enter the competition as

myself but Mr Philpott would not allow me to participate.

At last the bonfire was lit. People brought out chairs so they could sit around the blazing fire. Bottles and bottles of beer appeared and there was drink a-plenty. Dad came out of the house. He was smartly dressed and his face was animated in conversation. At moments like this I could feel the stirrings of affection for him but they were always short-lived, snuffed out by the Dad I knew too well behind the closed doors of 335.

Dad had trimmed the hedge into the shape of E.R. 1953 for the Coronation. I liked it better when Mom had shaped it to 335 but Dad's efforts at topiary made our hedge the most impressive in the lane. This success, and Dad's keenness as a gardener, persuaded most of the neighbours that he was a good man who occasionally got drunk to ease the burden of

> "A boy had a bag of marbles and gave me one to play with him. In the game, I won all his marbles and his bag, which made him cry. I gave him back most of the marbles, including his favourite one and the bag, as I didn't want his mother to come after me. Most of the remaining marbles, I exchanged for comics, leaving me enough to play with and win some more to obtain more comics."
>
> — A Child's Thoughts

looking after his children on his own.

Bernard and Brian came home for the coronation. From time to time they were allowed to stay with us for a few weeks. It was always good to see them, although they seemed to be content with their own company and made friends with children younger than me.

One pastime we all participated in was marbles. Boys who were given pocket money by their parents often bought themselves a bag of marbles but usually lost them to the Hicks boys! At one time, I must have had 150 marbles of all sizes and colours. Gambling and trading marbles kept me busy. I discovered that some of the children were happy to exchange comics for a few marbles. I won their marbles from them, and then returned them in exchange for comics! Before long, I had over fifty comics. Dad described me to an acquaintance as the 'Comic King'. I couldn't read the words on the comics, but I could follow some of the stories from the cartoon picture strips.

I made the cupboard that boxed in the gas meter in the corner of the living room into my desk and stored all my comics there. I would go over and over the

197

comics, often by candlelight, until slowly I began to recognise some of the words. I had always envied John his fountain pen and notebook. I had an open nib pen and a bottle of ink, probably taken from school, and I began to write out some of the words on scraps of paper. Before long, I found I could recognise them when I saw them again – I was able to read them. It was a tedious and primitive method but I began to learn some basic words, although it took years before I overcame my reading difficulties.

Superman and *Roy Rogers* were the titles of my favourite comics. I could hardly believe it when I heard that Roy Rogers and his famous horse, Trigger, were coming to the Birmingham Hippodrome Theatre. The Daily Mail ran a children's competition. The winner would meet Roy Rogers. I so much wanted to enter that competition and win! A young mother who lived down the road had a copy of the paper and very kindly sent off the form for me – but of course I didn't win. Many years later I was with some publishing friends in California. They

> "I have learned how to write some little words by copying them out of my comics. I have to copy them a lot of times, but I think I can learn words this way. It is hard and it takes a long time. I wish there was an easy way to learn to read and write."
>
> — A Child's Thoughts

198

had published some of Dale Rogers' (Roy's wife) books and I realised too late that I could have arranged to meet Roy Rogers personally, which would have fulfilled my childhood dream. I always regretted that I did not take that opportunity.

Each year the *Superman Annual* was published. It cost two shillings and sixpence and I decided I would save up for it. I mentioned it to Mrs Taylor next door and each time I had a few pennies, I gave them to her to save for me. Slowly, my savings reached one shilling and sixpence. Mrs Taylor put a deposit down to secure an annual for me but although I didn't get enough pennies to buy it, Mrs Taylor made up the difference and I got my prized possession.

Not having many things to call my own, the annual meant a lot to me. One day it disappeared. Neither my brothers or my sister ever owned up to taking it and its disappearance has remained a mystery. I find it hard to believe that Dad would actually have taken my annual to sell it for a few pennies in the pub to buy an extra drink, but it is possible.

As long as I was outdoors and nowhere near Dad, life at Bartley Green was full but that didn't prevent me from sinking deeper and deeper into myself. I found myself observing rather than joining in with the

199

other children. I was trying to make sense of what life was about. I developed an ability to look outside from the inside. I was constantly assessing and weighing up people, even the adults around me. It seemed to me that people accepted a sub-standard life, when there was so much more they could actually achieve. I did not want their sort of life for myself.

Although I still played with other children and occasionally went on an adventure trip with them, I spent more time on my own. On one such occasion, I had a profound encounter. Years later, I still wonder what it really meant.

I was alone and I had made myself a flimsy sword out of two pieces of stick held together with some twine. It was summer time and I was play-acting Robin Hood. My enemies were the wild yellow dandelions or their ripened flower heads which were transformed into snowy white parachutes.

> "I met a strange man in black today who took my sword of sticks out of my hand and turned it into a cross and then told me I would be a 'soldier of the cross'. He touched my head and blessed me. He had a gentle smile on his face. After this, he disappeared.
> I think he was an angel, but I don't understand why he was in black. I thought angels were always dressed in white."
>
> — A Child's Thoughts

200

I was walking towards the clay pits along a narrow dirt track with hedges on the left and fields bounded by fencing on the right. A strange man approached me from the opposite direction. He was dressed in long dark clothes. We lived in a small community where everybody knew everybody else and we seldom saw strangers, certainly not ones dressed like this man. I was apprehensive, but too much of a coward to turn and run. I stopped acting out the fantasy of defeating all my enemies and my sword dropped to my side. The man stopped in front of me, so I stopped. He spoke to me kindly.

'Son, what do you have in your hand?'

'A stick that I have made into a sword, but it's not a very good one,' I answered.

'Let me see it,' he said. I showed it to him and he took it out of my hand, holding its blade. Then he turned the sword with its handle upright and said, 'Son, this is not a sword. It is a cross and you are going to be a "Soldier of the Cross".' Having said this, he gave me back the sword. He softly laid his hand upon my head and blessed me, then walked away.

After I had taken a few slow steps, I turned around to take another look at this unusual man but he was no longer there. He had vanished. Maybe a longer time had elapsed than I realised and he had simply gone out of sight down the path but it was a strange incident

that stuck in my memory.

I have recounted this story to a few friends over the years and all of them have wondered whether the man who met me that day was an angel. If he was an angel, I cannot understand his dark clothes, unless that was a reflection of my own life at that time.

One thing the encounter taught me was that everything in life can be used for good or evil – even two twigs tied together. Furthermore, if something is going to be used for good, then there is often a sacrifice involved.

> "Part of me is glad that
> Mom's gone.
> If only Dad had gone too!
>
> Most of all, I wish,
> I wish I had a real Mom
> and Dad.
> I wish we were a real
> family.
> That's all.
>
> A real family."
>
> — A Child's Thoughts

CHAPTER 8
THE DEVIL'S WORK

CHAPTER 8
THE DEVIL'S WORK

I do not know what hurt me the most – his army belt, his fist, his feet, the early morning rousing from sleep and bed, the repeated interrogations, or simply the fact that for most of the time he ignored me, except when he wanted me to run an errand for him. My childhood memories are bruised with multiple abuse. I constantly try to ignore and forget them because they are so painful.

"Nobody sees us.
No-one looks at us.
No-one is interested
in us.

Behind closed doors,
it's another world
and no-one knows
or cares.

O dear!"

— A Child's Thoughts —

Would anything heal the anguish I felt when he forced me to walk the two-mile round trip to fetch his daily newspaper while he remained in bed after a late-night drinking session, knowing that I would be caned at school for being late? It was because he knew I'd be

punished and didn't care that hurt me long after the pain in my hand had ceased.

> "Please, Dad, don't delight in using the belt. Don't get satisfaction from hurting this child who is of your own seed."
>
> — A Child's Thoughts

If only he had looked at me and seen me as his son. But he never looked, therefore he never saw and never changed.

Children seem to have a natural instinct that tells them their fathers will protect and provide for them. If a father unjustly inflicts hurt on the child, the child suffers terrible insecurity. Mother had gone and my brothers and sisters were often away from home. I was on my own with Dad and I had every reason to plead that he would stop hurting me.

Can you imagine the terrifying sound he made with the army belt before he used it on me, the sting as the belt lashed the skin through thin clothing and the greater pain of realising that he seemed to delight in what he was doing? 'Dad! Stop it!' was a constant cry. It fell on deaf ears.

I wanted my father to stop the physical, mental, and emotional torment that cursed me psychologically throughout my days but I also wanted something else to stop. I wanted him to stop ignoring me as a person. I wanted Dad to recognise me as his son, not just as another pair of hands to run his errands and do his chores. I wanted to be valued by him, to be worth more than just the in Family Allowance money.

I wanted him to walk with me, to talk with me, to take me with him to the pictures and the park, to play football, to educate me and pass on to me the best rather than the worst of life. I wanted him to tell me stories and laugh with me, to pretend that my strength was as strong as his in the way that boys play with their fathers. I was not crying out for luxuries or expensive games or holidays – but for a 'Dad'. I longed deep down for a relationship from which respect could grow and friendship could develop. I have no roots that I am proud of, which is a curse I have to carry.

207

I think about these incidents with mixed emotions. Writing about the Devil's work – for the actions sprang from the heart of a man who demonstrated no fatherly understanding – is hard, fearfully hard. I have been dreading this section of my story. Why did we children never reveal to the outside world what was going on inside 335? Was it shame? Was it fear? Was it ignorance? Was it simply because we did not know that we could find genuine help if we unburdened ourselves? Whatever the reasons, I can feel that shame, fear and uncertainty again as I write.

Jean had left auntie and uncle in Sheffield and had been placed into care in Erdington Cottage Homes. Dad was supposed to pay something towards her keep, presumably her share of the Family Allowance. Bernard was living away, but Brian was at home with me, and John too from time to time.

One day, Dad brought a lady called Betty home with him. She was obviously his girlfriend. He occasionally brought acquaintances home, but they were usually men, drinking pals of his. One of them was an Irishman called Taffy who seemed to live on potatoes. Betty was an attractive, well-built woman. She must have been around fifteen years younger than Dad, and had a very happy, open personality. We children did not realise that she was a prostitute from Cardiff, a place Dad visited now and then. Before long Betty settled into the house and tried to turn over a new leaf. She started to decorate the room downstairs which was never used. Meanwhile Dad received a court summons because he'd not been paying towards Jean's keep. He had some money which he kept in his silver lighter box. I can remember him telling Betty where he had hidden the money so

> "Night after night, year in year out.
> Dad, drunk and cruel...
> so cruel.
> It hurts but no-one knows, nor must they."
>
> — A Child's Thoughts

that the police would not find it if they searched the house. He was obviously anticipating that, as on previous occasions, the magistrate would sympathise with his situation and be lenient. He hid the money just in case he got it wrong, and he did get it wrong. Dad went to prison for forty-two days.

Betty said she would look after us until Dad came out. She continued the decorating and moved Dad's bed downstairs. I think she had plans to decorate Dad's bedroom. She invited Brian and me to share the big bed with her

to help keep her warm but sometimes the summer nights were so hot that she slept with nothing on. Although by this time I was aware of the difference in boys and girls, the hormones that were supposed to kick start my physical and sexual development as I entered my teens were late developing. I am so glad. It proved to be my preservation! Although in the night I would feel her stroking me all over and encouraging me to return the stroking, it had no effect on me! Late at night, when she was particularly keen, I would simply fall straight into a deep sleep, happy to be in a quiet, calm house, with someone gentle in charge. Just to be near a mother figure while Dad was away was welcome. I never told anybody that Dad was in prison. Probably

I was too ashamed. It was a time when I was burdened with feelings of blame and shame.

Despite the lifestyle she had adopted, there were two sides to Betty. She had a kindness and a warmth about her that we had not seen before. She was happy to work in our home without making demands on us. We would do anything for her, and without Dad's presence there was a sense of calm and happiness. Before long Betty spent all the money Dad had hidden and then she changed. She may have intended to decorate Dad's bedroom, but his bed went back upstairs before any work was even started.

Then she came home with a man. He was a sailor and had one leg in a cast. It was summer. They spent a lot of time together in Dad's bedroom upstairs. Next came another man from the services. This one had an arm in a cast! Betty told us how sorry she felt for these injured men who had suffered in defence of our

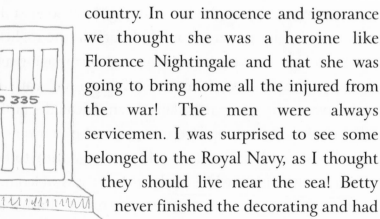

country. In our innocence and ignorance we thought she was a heroine like Florence Nightingale and that she was going to bring home all the injured from the war! The men were always servicemen. I was surprised to see some belonged to the Royal Navy, as I thought they should live near the sea! Betty never finished the decorating and had less and less time for us. Other men came to the house and rumours were rife. Yet again we children were being neglected.

Jean ran away from the Erdington Cottage Homes and found her way home. Betty was pleased to see her. I believe that when the authorities made enquiries about Jean's whereabouts, Betty lied and kept her hidden.

Things were getting out of hand. Our house was being used for prostitution, but thankfully it only went on for about a month. 335 was being used as a brothel and the neighbours had started to put two and two together.

> "Betty has changed. She was kind at first, while Dad was in prison and I felt noticed. Now she brings different men home at night with her and I am no longer noticed. Now I sleep on my own in the cold room again.
> I wish Betty had not changed."
>
> — A Child's Thoughts

When I talked to my mother decades later she told me that there had been rumours that she had used her rooms in the slums for the purpose of prostitution. Now I wonder whether it was rumour or fact. Mother was always desperate to acquire more money, and from time to time she did buy some expensive looking clothes. Was history now repeating itself? Was Dad's repeated reference to mother as a whore a reflection of

211

the truth, or of the sordid life that he was living, or of both?

One evening Betty dressed Jean up, put make-up on her face and took her to Birmingham city centre. Jean came home but we never saw Betty again. Like mom, she deserted us. We didn't understand what was happening and I felt sad that she had gone. When she was living with us Dad was not so violent. We weren't tormented with incessant questioning in the early hours of the morning. Unlike mother, Betty had a happy nature.

> "I envy Jean coming home because Betty is now giving her all the attention and is dressing her up to take her to see the big lights in the city."
>
> — A Child's Thoughts

Jean said that Betty had gone with two men, leaving her alone at night in Birmingham with no money for the fare home. She wandered around the city for hours looking for Betty, then eventually started the twelve-mile walk back to Bartley Green. Two gentlemen, seeing she was distressed, escorted her to the bus and made sure she was taken all the way home. They were her guardian angels, protecting a vulnerable young girl from potential harm.

There were no guardian angels living inside 335 Stonehouse Lane. Evil deeds were bound up with

Dad's dark secrets when he made those trips to Cardiff. Maybe the reason why Dad came home in the small hours of the morning, rather than late at night, was because he was spending his money and the Family Allowance not only on drink but also on prostitutes. If Dad had such dark secrets, they were unknown to us.

Betty was gone. She was not our mother and she didn't have to stay. But in those moments when she had cared for us, she had symbolised what I wanted from a mother. Her departure reopened old wounds. Although I could not articulate my feelings, I realise now that I felt useless, helpless and valueless. Betty had gone somewhere. I was going nowhere.

Since Dad was in prison and Betty had left, we children were sent into care yet again.

Jean went back to Erdington Cottage Homes and I went to Middlemore Homes. Brian and Bernard were sent elsewhere. I still attended the same senior school. One lunchbreak I decided to miss lunch and go back to 335 with a schoolmate to show him where I lived. I was amazed to find Dad there. He had just been released from prison. He cried. It was the only time I had ever seen Dad crying. He took me in his arms and hugged me. It felt so strange. Then he sent me to the shop for some cigarettes, a tin of Irish stew and a

213

ROBERT HICKS

bar of chocolate to share with the boy who was with me. I knew he could not afford it, so I refused to buy the chocolate but fetched the other things he wanted. When I thought about it later, I realised that Dad had offered to buy me something I had wanted ever since Donald stole my bar of chocolate so many years earlier. We had to get back to school, so we only stopped a few minutes. Dad was still very emotional. He had gambled on Betty being there when he came home. I expect she had made many promises to him. The fact that he had left her in the house with his money was his way of saying he trusted her. Now he had come home to no money, no Betty, no children. Seeing me had brought it all into the open. Dad was in his forties. Would this experience make him realise what his children had been suffering for so many years?

> "Dad came out of prison and hugged me and cried. It was strange to be hugged by Dad. It has never happened before. I feel sorry for Dad, but it's his own fault that he went into prison.
> I never told anyone that my Dad was in prison."
> — A Child's Thoughts

On the way back to school, my pal said how handsome my Dad was and how kind it was of him to offer us chocolate. After school I returned to Middlemore Homes hoping that maybe, just maybe, Dad would change. But he didn't change. Instead

214

things went from bad to worse. My dear sister, Jean, suffered most.

Jean was in her early mid teens and Dad was beginning to depend on her to do his cooking, cleaning and ironing. On one occasion, she made a mistake when pressing his trousers and put creases in the sides instead of the front and back. He went berserk.

Each of us failed to achieve the standard of ironing Dad required and were subject to his instant violent reactions.

Jean was changing, physically. From being a little girl she was turning into a young woman. She still felt that she was unlovable because of the squint in her eyes, the way Dad terrorised her and the fact that her mother had deserted her. At this time in her life none of her brothers understood her and when she most needed her mother's care, or at least that of a neighbour or friend, she had none. All she had was Dad who had just finished a prison sentence for refusing to pay her keep. Why Dad left us in the care of a prostitute while he was in jail remains a mystery. Perhaps he thought he could start a new life with her. If so, he must have been out of his mind

According to Jean, one day

215

Dad came home drunk and she cooked his food while we were asleep upstairs. There was no money for the gas meter and the supply ran out. The house was in darkness. In the dark Dad crudely raped dear Jean. My heart is full of tears and tenderness for my sister, as I write these words. I wonder whether I should include this horrible part of the story, yet I realise there are many others who suffer abuse and they need to know that there is hope for the future and friends who will help. Jean always wanted to love and be loved but she would never ever consent to such debauchery. She felt confused, cheated and defiled – and so she was. Dad vomited all over her and Jean had to clean herself up. Dad's violence and cruelty to his children reached its nadir in this most wicked and evil action. He threatened to kill Jean if she told anybody and she believed he meant it. My own emotions, as I write, are in turmoil. To think that we were asleep upstairs while this was taking place downstairs, and on other occasions in Dad's bedroom. To think that we would suffer less bullying at such a price – I can't get my mind round such evil. It seems

> "Jean is never happy and she is always crying and no-one understands her. She keeps running away, but always comes back. I feel sorry for her being the only girl at home."
>
> — A Child's Thoughts

216

that 335 was void of God, love and humanity. This was the Devil's work if ever anything was.

Having committed the vile deed and obtained Jean's silence, Dad purged his conscience by giving her little treats, like taking her to the pictures. But then he would repeat the violation. Jean, a girl in her early teens, should have been dreaming of her future life, of the possibilities of boyfriends, romance, courtship, engagement, marriage, motherhood – the rightful inheritance of every young woman. She was robbed of all this. Yet, painful though it would be, she did manage to put the past behind her. She found love and motherhood and her children and grandchildren are rightfully proud of her.

Once, I was surprised to see Jean coming out of Dad's bedroom. He told me that she had spent the night there because she was cold, but they had had a blanket between them. At the time I accepted this simple explanation. Dad must have known he would be sent to prison if the police found out what he was doing to his only daughter.

Even if we boys had known, I am not sure we would have been brave enough to have gone to the police. There was an unwritten law that the awful things that happen in a family behind closed doors must not

become the business of the police. I am not at all sure what action we would have taken. Many years passed before I learnt the truth, and if Dad had still been alive I am sure I would have done something about it. If Jean had agreed to my taking action, I wonder what the consequences would have been. Listening to the stories of other people who have tried to secure proper sentencing through the courts, the only way to gain justice means becoming a victim all over again.

Having been abused by Dad, Jean was sent back to Erdington Cottage Homes. Later she returned to 335. By now, she realised she was losing out in every aspect of her life and she became deeply depressed. She decided, along with the rest of us that she would kill Dad. I did not take her seriously, but if I had known what Dad was subjecting her to, maybe I would have done. The plan was to turn on the gas supply to the fire in his bedroom when he was asleep, making sure the window and door were closed and all the gaps were sealed with blankets. We agreed that we would make sure we had enough money to put in the meter to purchase enough gas to do the deed.

We talked about this in detail, but I thought we were only play-acting. I know now that Jean was serious, very serious indeed. Jean has told me that the only reason she did not push us to carry out the plan was because one of Dad's eyelids remained partly open

when he was asleep and we might think he was able to see us! This peculiarity saved him from an attempt on his life by his daughter who longed for his love but hated his abuse.

One evening I came in from the fields. Brian was nursing his leg. Every inch of it was covered in bruises. His leg had swollen and turned blue. Brian couldn't remember the cause of Dad's wrath, but he remembered what had happened to his leg. There was a brass fender in front of the fireplace. The centre section was loose to allow for a larger fireplace to be fitted. Dad had taken out the loose section of the fender and hit Brian across the leg again and again and again. When I saw Brian I was petrified, because I realised that one day Dad would do it to me too. It played on my mind most nights as I lay in the dark waiting to hear Dad bang the back door as he came in. When Brian was sent to a remand home as punishment for some petty offence, he was relieved to be outside Dad's control.

> "Jean said we should turn the gas on in Dad's bedroom when he is asleep. I don't know whether she means it. Things would be happier if Dad was not here and we belonged to a good family."
>
> — A Child's Thoughts

219

Dad made Brian swear on his life that if anyone asked about his leg he would say he had fallen off his

ROBERT HICKS

bike. Brian was questioned and he did lie even though he did not have a bike and could not ride one. I find it incredible that the schoolteachers could not see for themselves that Brian was neglected. They only had to look at his clothes, the wild habits he had developed and the problems he had with speech. When they saw his leg so bruised and battered, they must have realised that he was also being abused, and they should have notified the authorities! But things were different then and perhaps the probation officers' records would belie the truth with their references to a clean house and a congenial father who was finding it difficult to bring up his family single-handed. Whatever the reason, dad again escaped being punished for the cruelty he meted out to his children.

> "I cannot believe what I have seen today. Brian's leg doesn't look like a boy's leg any more. I am afraid that someone is going to get killed."
>
> — A Child's Thoughts

I can never remember feeling secure or happy. I was tempted to run away many times but my experience with the police and the promise I made when the constable returned me to my father stopped me.

The Devil was at work in the house every time mother stayed out all evening or all night, leaving us defenceless in the face of Dad's anger.

THE DEVIL'S WORK

The Devil was at work in the house when we children were forced to wash floors, polish lino and clean the cast-iron fireplace.

The Devil's work was to make children not yet into their teens cook food, wash their own clothes and occasionally launder the sheets to go back on the bed that same night.

The Devil's work was poverty – needless poverty because both Dad and Mom were working. Even when Dad was off work with a bad back he still got dole money, and any extra money Mom earned was spent on new clothes for her.

The Devil's work was to inflict asthma on two of my brothers, to leave a boy and a girl feeling inferior and suffering ridicule because they had squints in their eyes, while children in other families had corrective medical help.

The Devil's work was to isolate Bernard when he was sent to convalescent school and was abandoned by his family. For two years he never received a letter, a card or a visit.

The Devil's work was to tear the children apart when Donald, the eldest brother, the James Bond of the family, was unjustly put on probation, then sent

221

away for discipline before going into the army.

The Devil's work was to ensure that John's potential was not developed or encouraged as it would have been in other families. If Donald was the James Bond of the family, then John was the Errol Flynn, always making an impression on girls from near and far.

The Devil's work was to prevent Jean from developing through her teenage years into womanhood and union in marriage in a natural way.

The Devil's work was to make me feel smaller and smaller in my own estimation until in the end I felt a non-person, with no worth. It flowed like a polluted river, pouring into my soul and spirit and cursing each day that I lived.

The Devil's work was for us to have two half-sisters whom we would never see grow up and develop or even be aware of. To this day I have no idea what they made of their lives.

The Devil's work was to make a mockery of the text hanging on the wall about the 'Perfect Friend' who knows the best and worst about us and loves us all the same. It mocked me so often, though there came a time when that same text would express the miracle in my own life as its truth filtered deep into my emotions.

When I say 'the Devil's work' I am not thinking of a monster with tail and horns, with a hollow grin on his face, holding a toasting fork in one hand. The Devil I speak of is the culture and the system that allows all these things to happen – that allows a father and mother to act cruelly and without compassion towards their children. Both mother and father were doing the Devil's work and had been doing it from the time that they brought their children into the world and refused to accept the responsibility of parenting them with love and encouragement or to nurture them as people within a real world. Later I realised that this happens in all sections of society and to many children from all walks of life. Regardless of their background, there are children who are denied the sacrificial love of parents, whose care is not the first priority. Indeed I discovered that as life in the post-war years became more sophisticated and materialistic, the attack on family life and on the relationship between parents and children would grow ever stronger. When I became a parent, I was determined to avoid falling into the same trap. Whenever I over-reacted to an incident involving one of my children, my soul was in torment lest history should repeat itself.

Before I broke free of the Devil's work at 335 I learnt from other experiences that there was a much bigger world than that of Bartley

> "I know what is happening at home is not normal. I know it is not good. I know it is all wrong.
> If only I knew what to do. One day I will."
>
> — A Child's Thoughts

Green, even though that too was expanding. I began to discover this bigger world at a time when I was changing from a child into a youth. I recognised that one day I would have to face up to my greatest fear. That was when I had to do something that went against all my instincts and was far removed from my nature.

CHAPTER 9

DISCOVERING A BIGGER WORLD

CHAPTER 9

DISCOVERING A
BIGGER WORLD

As I reached my mid-teens, my biological clock told me that my wild days among the fields, streams and trees were coming to an end. The open spaces were losing their appeal.
Physically my growth

> "Ripples from a stone thrown in the reservoir are not content to stay by the stone, but ripple out until they reach the edge of their world...
> I feel the same!"
>
> — A Child's Thoughts

was slow, but it was happening and I was becoming increasingly aware of the wider world.

One day at school Mr Woolley called a group of boys to the front of the class. He had seen them experimenting with their new-found sexual awareness. He sent them to the headmaster and grinned as he did so, as though it was a big joke. I thought they were going to be caned, but apparently they had a lesson about 'the birds and the bees' which became a source of amusement to everyone.

ROBERT HICKS

At the time I did not understand what all the fuss was about. One of the boys, who seemed more precocious than the others, boasted of his exploits with various girls. Again, I had no idea what he was talking about.

I was slowly changing and maturing but I was worried because I was not sure what I was changing into. I was becoming restless, and the joy of abandonment that had hitherto been my salvation no longer held the same charm.

I believe that emotionally I had already grown up, even though I felt insecure. I was more aware of things around me than other children of my age and I could read people's moods and interpret by their body language and the look on their faces what they were thinking or feeling. Maybe I had spent too much time observing Dad and this had sharpened those skills.

As I grew up, I realised that nobody really wanted me, understood me or enjoyed having me around just because I was me. I became dissatisfied, disgruntled, frustrated and irritable, but it had no effect on anyone else, for the simple reason that no-one else had any interest in me. The days were fast drawing to a close when I dreamt of being Superman with incredible powers, or Roy Rogers astride his famous

228

horse Trigger, caught up in a constant battle against the baddies. Those days were over. New days were coming.

Where was I to go? What was I to do? What would become of me? What would happen? All these questions swirled around in my mind and they seemed to be pushing me to the point where I would have to make a decision and accept responsibility for my life and my future. Whatever was taking place within, outwardly I was still a small boy in short trousers, barely five feet tall, with an active but undisciplined mind and emotions that were battered and bruised.

Teenage years can be difficult at the best of times, and the outcome of those years is extremely difficult to predict. In addition to all the teenage confusion, tension and uncertainty that was going on in my life, I was also being made to look and feel an idiot. There seemed little room for optimism and yet I had not given up hope. I knew that if I could take control of my own life, I just might stand a chance.

"Everything around me is alive, but I don't feel as if I am living. Everything around me is growing. Why am I not growing? It will be a long time before I leave school; maybe then I will start to live and grow. I do very much want to grow as I feel very small."

— A Child's Thoughts

229

I talked to some of the older girls from the other half of the school occasionally. They seemed so much more grown up and self-assured than me and had a sense of destiny about them. This also contributed to the feeling that I was not in control of my life and would never really grow up unless I gained that control.

A long, hard, slow road into that bigger world lay ahead but I had to overcome a major obstacle before the spark of optimism within me could be fanned into a flame.

230

Birmetals, a new factory built in the war years to provide metals for Birmingham was half an hour's walk from us. It was a 'shadow factory' which meant that its location was kept secret to prevent it becoming a target for German bombers. My discovery of a much bigger world during my teenage years started with an event at Birmetals. I was twelve or thirteen when I found out that there was going to be a summer fete in the grounds opposite Birmetals and it was going to be a huge affair. The entrance ticket cost a few pennies. I didn't have any money but I managed to get in without a ticket! The funfair was nothing like the mini-Disneyworld at Bellevue which I visited on that fateful day when I discovered Mom's affection for another man. There were several stalls selling everything from homemade cakes, jams and pickles to tools, pots and pans and second hand goods. Other stalls offered games of

chance to the hundreds of people who came to the fair that day.

Before long I reached a huge marquee. It was crowded inside with people sitting at dozens of small tables being served tea and cakes by young men and young girls in attractive clean aprons. One of the smartly-dressed young men stopped me as I wandered around the huge tent in some kind of a daze. He could see I had no money and he made sure I was escorted out and told not to come back in!

231

I was soon caught up in the excitement of people winning or losing in the games of chance. Two or three people were serving on nearly all the stalls but one stall had only a single person running it. The stall was not the most attractive. It featured a pyramid of tin cans. For a few pennies people received three tennis balls and the chance to knock down the tins. If they succeeded they won a surprise gift. The stallholder was constantly bending down to pick up the balls and reassembling the pyramid. Some people got bored waiting for their turn and walked away, so I offered to help and my offer was accepted. I really enjoyed myself. People came to the stall, noticed me and got a big smile in return, the sort of smile that came naturally to me whenever I was away from home

and doing something worthwhile and being accepted for doing it. I can still see some of those people in my mind's eye and the disappointment or excitement on their faces.

At midday everybody went off to eat the picnics they had brought with them or to buy lunch in the huge marquee. Tommy Jones, the man I'd been working with, told me it was time for a lunch-break. I was amazed that he left me in sole charge while he went away for lunch. He trusted me. It had never happened before. When I saw him go towards the marquee I realised that when my lunch-break came I wouldn't have any money for food. I decided to increase the profitability of the stall. Most people were having lunch and there were only a few still going around the stalls. My scheme was to help the punters knock down the tins so that instead of one in ten players winning, one in every four or five would win. A crowd soon built up around the stall. By the time Mr Jones got back from lunch I had ten shillings in one pocket and a half-crown in the other! Tommy Jones was thrilled when I tipped the ten shillings into his hands. He gave me one shilling as pay and a free ticket for lunch in the big marquee. He had probably intended all along to provide me with a lunch ticket but he hadn't told me. Feeling ten feet tall I strode into the large marquee and relished the opportunity to make sure

that the smart attendant who had expelled me a few hours earlier served me!

The sheer excitement of that day, plus the shilling in one pocket and half-crown in the other and the special treat of lunch in the big marquee erased any memory of what was on my plate!

While I was in the big tent I realised I still had the half-crown in my pocket. If Mr Jones hadn't given me the

"When I have free school dinner tickets, I feel bad and very poor. But today I have an official 'pass' into the big marquee for a meal that I have earned by working at the fun day and I feel great!
I have never felt like this before with a meal ticket. It is wonderful!"

— A Child's Thoughts

233

lunch ticket and shilling I have no doubt that I would have kept it but I responded to his generosity and fairness by telling him that I had forgotten to give him the rest of his money. To my utter amazement and bewilderment he told me to keep it. I worked on his stall through the afternoon although he closed quite early having passed his target as a result of my initiative while he was at lunch. That day I learnt a very simple lesson about people and business. If you want customer response you have to give them something which they believe is a fair deal. A one in ten chance is nothing compared to one in four or five.

With so much money in my pocket, I was able

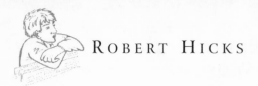

afford to do something I had always dreamt of doing –
to go to the Royalty Picture House in Harborne, where
poor people seldom went. I can not remember which
film I saw. I took pleasure in the fact that I, Bobby
Hicks, had earned the money that enabled me to be
there.

A few months after the fair, Christmas was
approaching and I had no money at all. I tried to think
of a way we children could earn some money. Mr
Taylor did not want horse manure at that time of year.
Most of the people who occasionally allowed me to
take their empty bleach or pop bottles back to the local
shop in exchange for the deposit on them, were
themselves saving every penny they could for
Christmas. The situation was getting desperate. With
only a few days to Christmas we had no money for
anything at all, not even for a ticket to the pictures.

Bernard, Brian and I were hanging around the
Weoley Castle pub when I suggested that we try carol
singing. We began to sing as loudly as we could outside
the main door of the pub, not knowing whether
anybody could hear because of the babble on the
inside. A man near the entrance heard us and opened
the door. He told everyone to be quiet and invited us
in to sing. As we only knew one verse we had to repeat
it two or three times, which was more than enough for
our audience. The man took off his cap and everyone

in the pub put their loose change into it. He emptied the coins into a dirty handkerchief and handed it over to me. We could not believe our good fortune! When we got outside we counted it. It came to over ten shillings. We shared it between the three of us, but I felt that as I had come up with the idea I should have half and Bernard and Brian a quarter each. They did not complain and that night we went to the pictures and treated ourselves to fish and chips!

Christmas came and went and a new year dawned – 1954. It was a year during which the Americans launched the world's first nuclear-powered submarine. It weighed an incredible 3108 tons and its nuclear reactor heated the water to produce steam to drive its turbines. The submarine could stay submerged for months at a time and travel indefinitely at nearly twenty-five miles an hour. That same year, America exploded its second hydrogen bomb and the fear of a nuclear war began to spread throughout the world. In Britain we thrilled to

> "Today, the big lady from the N.S.P.C.C. came again with trousers, shirt, coat, mac and shoes for me. As usual, they are all too big and she tells me that I will grow into them. I know they will be worn out before I grow into them and I'll probably lose the mac. I wish I had some proper clothes just for me."
> — A Child's Thoughts

235

the news of Roger Bannister's record-breaking four-minute mile, we read of Marilyn Monroe's marriage and danced to Bill Haley and the Comets hit song, 'Rock around the Clock'. World and national events, however, were of little concern to me.

It was in the late autumn of 1954 and near the end of term. I was told a lady from the NSPCC was coming to school. She was going to examine me and a few other children in an empty classroom. The other children were already stripped to their pants and vests and when the lady asked me to take off my shirt and shorts I blushed red with shame as I explained that I did not wear any underclothes. I stood in the queue to be examined, still dressed in my shorts and shirt, yet I felt that, of all the children I was the only one who was undressed. I recognised the NSPCC lady immediately. She was a big woman with a heaving bosom and a happy, relaxed face. The previous year she had given me a few clothes and a raincoat. I had lost the raincoat soon afterwards and I wondered whether I'd be questioned about the loss. She looked into my ears and eyes, checked my throat, listened to my chest and then really embarrassed me by opening my trousers to see if everything inside them was normal!

While I put my shirt back on, she told me to sit by her desk while she made some notes. I told her who I was and where I lived and that my mother had run

away some years earlier. She listened to me intently and spoke to me softly. She asked whether I had ever been on a holiday. I told her no. Next she enquired whether I had ever been on a steam train. I had seen them pass nearby when I was in the Erdington Cottage Homes but I had never ridden in one. Then she asked whether I had ever seen the sea and again I said no, although once at school in an art class I had drawn what I thought the sea would look like. My picture portrayed huge waves dashing against the rocks, dark clouds and flashes of lightning. The English teacher, who also taught art, praised me for my imagination, although I suspect the drawing was poor.

237

The kind-faced lady from the NSPCC, whom I would have gladly had for my mother, then talked about the others in my family and wrote down Bernard and Brian's names. She asked whether I would mind being away from home for Christmas. I told her that nothing would give me greater joy! When school closed for the Christmas holidays a few weeks later, father received a letter from the NSPCC. Arrangements had been made for Bernard, Brian and myself to spend Christmas in a large house at Weston-Super-Mare!

Dad pretended that he was making a real sacrifice to pay for us all to go away on holiday and have the

best Christmas ever. Actually, the magnificent NSPCC and their voluntary supporters covered all the costs. Dad made no contribution at all. When the time came for us to go, Dad didn't give us a penny other than the fare to New Street railway station, a place we'd never been before. I am not sure if Auntie Lily took us or one of the neighbours, or whether we made our own way there, but Dad definitely did not take us.

I was used to living in the quiet countryside. New Street station at Christmas time, with hundreds of people dashing in all directions and the roar of the mighty engines with steam billowing from them, the hooting, and the hissing was overpowering! It was a wonder-world.

> "I am on a train for the first time. It's a train with a big powerful engine full of life, pulling lots and lots of carriages carrying so many people – and I am one of them! I can't believe it."
>
> — A Child's Thoughts

We had been told to meet at the station in good time to ensure that no-one was left behind, so we had plenty of time to watch the trains arriving and departing from the station. The memory of that first time on a station platform will stay with me for ever.

I had seen steam engines in films at the pictures, roaring through vales and tunnels but nothing I had seen in the films prepared

me for being so close to the trains on that exciting day.

At last we boarded a train with strict instructions not to put our heads out of the windows. We were each given a packed lunch – sandwiches, a piece of cake and an apple. Whenever the council or a charity provided a lunch, it always had the same welcome constituents and the apple was usually a delicious Cox's Orange Pippin. The children with the NSPCC travelled together in designated carriages. The train slowly pulled out of the station and began to build up speed. We passed through built-up areas then fields dotted with sheep and cows, more buildings and factories and then mile after mile of countryside. I had never been so far away from Birmingham. I began to realise there was a huge world, even bigger than the miracle world of Bartley Green. Although we had been instructed not to put our heads out of the windows, we couldn't resist it! I was seeing the countryside in a way that I'd never seen it before. We soon had faces blackened with soot and eyes full of grit! We ran along the corridor to wash and came back to do it all over again.

Each carriage had one long corridor with small compartments for six or eight passengers leading off it. The seats were large and luxurious. People who built those

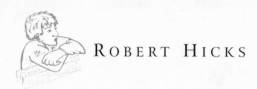

early carriages really knew how to make their customers comfortable. When the train entered a tunnel the excitement was tangible. There was a hoot of the horn, the hiss as surplus steam was cleared away, then everything went black and the sound of the train changed. Very few were brave enough to put their heads out of the windows, but those who did saw the daylight at the end of the tunnel getting bigger and bigger until the train shot like a bullet out of it.

> "The train is alive and it talks to itself over and over again, as well as making funny noises when it goes through the tunnels. It goes so fast. I can't believe I am really on this train!"
>
> — A Child's Thoughts

We gobbled up our packed lunches in no time at all. In our excitement, we ran up and down the corridors despite the NSPCC leaders who were in charge of us and tried to restrain our exuberance.

The fantastic journey, which probably lasted two or three hours, ended all too quickly. For the first time ever I was in a seaside town. We alighted at the much smaller railway station of Weston-Super-Mare, which lacked the noise and excitement of New Street Birmingham. Even the air smelt different. I was not sure whether I liked it or not.

For much of the year, the tide at Weston-Super-Mare goes a long way out, leaving a wide stretch of

sandy beach. This Christmas the tide was in, right up to the sea wall. We could smell the saltiness in the air – such a contrast to the country air of the green fields at home.

The person in charge let us go to see the sea on our way to the big house where we were staying. I couldn't believe my eyes. A stone wall formed the boundary between the road and the beach. Not far off was a pier reaching into the sea. Waves smashed against the wall and the pier. They seemed to be a hundred feet high! Of course I was only small and the waves may have been quite modest, but to me they were immense. I was mesmerised. My mouth dropped open and my feet refused to move. All I could do was stand and look. I was told to move forward with the other boys but I was so transfixed that an adult had to come and take me by the hand. I had heard about the sea in school. I had even painted a picture of what I thought it looked like, but to see it with my own eyes, to be part of it all was amazing.

There have been a few times in my life when I have been mesmerised, feeling powerless to do anything other than stand and stare – when I flew by helicopter into the Grand Canyon, when I felt the force of the great Niagara Falls viewed at water level from a boat trip, when I was taking photographs in Arizona's Death Valley and when I was visiting the Rockies and got caught up in an electric storm. But even these and other dramatic experiences which have left me rooted to the spot cannot compare to the force of the wind upon my young face, the smell of the salt in the air, and the vision of giant waves bursting on the walls of Weston-Super-Mare!

We arrived at the big house at the top of a steep hill. Having walked from the railway station, and being unused to climbing hills, we all had aching leg muscles. The door swung open and a tall man with striking features beckoned us in with a huge smile and a warm welcome to share Christmas with him!

Most of the children were Bernard and Brian's age. I was one of the older ones, if not the oldest. Although I was small for my years, I was a little taller than the others.

> "I am fourteen and grown up, but today I feel like a little child. Here at the seaside I am smelling, feeling and seeing things I have never seen before. I feel fixed to the spot with excitement! I never knew the sea was so big, so powerful! It has touched me ... I have felt it and tasted it. It is now inside me and will never leave me."
>
> — A Child's Thoughts

Mr Noble, for that was his name, must have read my face because he said, 'This is your first Christmas by the sea, is it not?' It was my first real Christmas, never mind being by the sea! It was a Christmas I

would never forget.

A pattern was soon established. When the tide was out we were allowed to go down to the beach and play amongst the rocks and sand without supervision. It would not happen today but people were more trusting and children were used to playing out alone in the 1950's.

I found a small cave amongst the rocks. We were told that nobody had ever entered it. To get in you would have to crawl on hands and knees and I was sure a little boy could manage it. But the cave was dangerous because once the tide came in it was submerged and a child trapped inside would drown. I went in two or three times but I suffered nightmares in which I was trying to get out of the small opening as the waves swamped the cave. Once I was playing under the pier when the sea came in fast. I had to run for it and lost one of my shoes. I was afraid to go back to the house with only one shoe, so I plunged into the water and searched until I found it, which was a foolish thing to do. That experience also gave me nightmares for months to come.

We took a packed lunch with us every day but had to be back in the afternoon because our cooked meal was served early. We always had hot food in the evening, including a pudding, which was usually a sponge with custard. Sometimes the sponge had jam

243

on it, or marmalade or steamed with raisins or currants, but I liked it best when it came smothered in treacle or syrup. We were given a hot drink at night-time and went to bed early.

Each evening, between the meal and bedtime, Mr Noble taught us some carols. It was the first time that I heard in full the nativity story of the first Christmas, of how God became man, conceived of a virgin, and entered our world to save us from our sins. Mr Noble was almost certainly a Christian and on the Sunday we all went to church. As we had worked hard at our singing, arrangements were made for us to sing at one of the local hotels where retired people from the Forces spent their Christmas. I was told that I had been chosen to sing a solo verse in the carol, 'We three kings'. I was glad it was only one verse. I couldn't read so I had to memorise the words. The time came and we were led down the long hill and across the town to the hotel for servicemen and women. I did my best with the solo, but I think I was out of tune most of the time.

A collection was made for the children at the end. I was upset by the audience's lack of generosity and puzzled that the poor people in the pub at home had given as much as the people in this posh hotel. We received a few pennies each but Mr Noble gave me an extra threepenny bit for singing the solo.

On Christmas Day we each received a present!

Most of the children were given a wind-up metal toy –
a car, a bicycle and even a fire engine on which the
firemen went up one side of the ladder and down the
other. Because I was older, I was given a pair of roller-
skates. I was very disappointed. My brother John had
once had a tin toy and I had envied him. I tried the
roller-skates on the wooden floor in the hall of the big
house, but was not successful
with them. My heart was on
the wind-up tin toys. To my
surprise, the boy with the fire
engine wanted to do an
exchange. I didn't need any
persuasion but I felt a little
embarrassed when Mr Noble
found out. The tin toy broke
while I was still on holiday,

> "I am happy in this big
> house by the sea. The
> days are going by too
> fast. I don't want the
> holiday to end. It is a real
> Christmas: my first real
> Christmas ever."
> — A Child's Thoughts

245

and I did not even bring it home. I wished I had kept
the roller-skates!

The funfair stall, the carol singing at the pub and
Christmas by the sea introduced me to a world outside
335 Stonehouse Lane. Each helped to sow the seeds of
rebellion against the sub-standard life I was living at
home. Together with my father's cruelty, so evident in
the incident with Brian's battered leg, they strength-
ened my resolve to break free from the awful life I was
living. Slowly but steadily my determination grew.

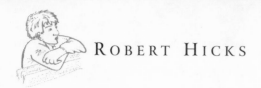
When I look at my brothers and sister, I feel that their lives and victories are stories worth telling. Jean, Bernard and Brian were gentle people who wouldn't want to hurt anybody. John had an abundance of natural talent. Donald eventually escaped from Dad by going into Borstal care and then into the army. He died from diabetes in his fifties, leaving behind his wife, Janice, and a family that he was immensely proud of.

> "Dad keeps kicking Lassie, and she crawls up to him with her eyes wide open, pleading for him to stop.
> Dad's cruel to her. Just because she wet the kitchen floor, Dad threw her out of the house.
> I can still hear her whining outside the door. I wish Dad would stop kicking Lassie - it makes me hurt inside."
>
> — A Child's Thoughts

The day when I saw Brian's beaten, shattered leg, I resolved to fight Dad, to stand up to him, so I could escape the cruel, cruel, pain he had inflicted on the youngest member of the family. I can't recall how long it took for this determination to harden, but by the time I left school and was about to start work as an errand boy for a local family grocer, the seed was sown. I was determined! I kept saying to myself, 'I must fight! I must fight! I MUST FIGHT!'

CHAPTER 10
THE FIGHT

THE FIGHT

I had lived with a multitude of fears, most of them related to my father. An element of fear can be good for a child if it comes from a sense of right and wrong and an understanding of the fairness of fatherly discipline. My fear of Dad had nothing to do with right and wrong or the development of a good conscience through love and respect. It was a fear that turned to hate over the years.

> "What is love?
> It is not just a feeling
> Or just caring,
> Or just talking.
>
> It is being there all the time. That's why people get married ... at least, I thought so."
>
> — A Child's Thoughts

249

I must choose my words carefully. To say that I hated my father is to admit that the very process of nature had been reversed. Although raging hatred between father and son is not unknown, it is not the norm but an exception. For me to confess that I was beginning to hate my father is to admit that emotionally something foreign to me was developing. I realise that some people have a capacity for such a negative emotion, one that in the end becomes a vice. Later in my life some of my own emotions would plague me but hate is not one of them. I am not aware of hating anyone. Yet what I felt towards my father was turning into hate.

> "I want to love my Dad and to honour and respect him. I want to be proud of him. I want other people to know I have a good father. I wish... but I know that wishing is no good."
>
> — A Child's Thoughts

It was not the physical abuse, terrible though that was, that left lasting pain but the hurt of realising that he never wanted to get to know me, not even in a casual way. To him, I was a nobody. I simply did not exist. I feel sure that if the Government had not given him some money in the form of Family Allowance or additional dole money, it would have made no difference to him whether I existed or not. I hated him for that.

I hated him because he was only concerned about his own clothes and his own appearance and never mine. I hated him for the way he lived a double life as far as the neighbours were concerned. I hated him because he never gave me the love he should have given or made any effort to be a good father to me. Fear gradually turned into hate over the years. My mother

had poisoned and destroyed any affection that might have developed between our father and us. My father destroyed not only affection, but respect as well. My father and my mother lost both their good name and their honour a long time before they died.

On the day I fought Dad I looked into his soul. For the first time our eyes locked and the fear that had turned into hate turned again, this time into pity. I have seen the expression that begs for mercy in the faces of animals and people, especially when someone far more powerful than them crushes them until nothing is left. My father used his superior strength against me and my siblings and even the family dog. I never thought I would see such a plea for mercy in my father's eyes, but I did and in that split second when our eyes met and I looked into his soul, every ounce of hate within me evaporated. So I was doubly victorious! I overcame both fear and hate and was left with pity alone.

For the past ten years I had learnt not to cry aloud but to cry inwardly and silently. Now in my teenage years my crying was of a different kind and it felt more painful. I was grieving and pining for a lost childhood, carrying into adulthood the pain and the longing that life might not continue along the same course. The fields of Bartley Green could no longer soothe the pain. I grieved for my life which had been destroyed and longed for comfort, but the wind in the trees, the birds in the sky, the horses in the fields and the whole voice of the countryside which surrounded me could not bring healing. It was difficult changing from a child to a young man. I was hurting in a way I had never experienced before. The time would soon come when I had to start work as an errand boy. At least I would earn a weekly wage.

> "I know so much...
> but I also know so little.
> What I don't know is
> more important than
> what I do know.
> I am ashamed,
> but I must try to learn
> what I don't yet know."
> — A Child's Thoughts

Except on those few occasions I have mentioned I had no money. Apart from free meals at school and proper food in the institutions, my life had generally been without nourishment. Except for the times when the NSPCC or institutions had given me clothes to wear and shoes for my feet, I had not been suitably clothed.

I slowly became aware that I was a male and that females were different to males. I had only perceived females in terms of good and bad mothers but my hormones were telling me that there was more to the

opposite sex than that.

In spite of my lack of formal education at school, I had learnt a thousand things through observation that stirred my imagination and made me aware of life in its raw state, things that educated children would take many years to appreciate. If true education is preparation for life, then I had received a fair education, but the society I was part of considered me to be unqualified as

253

far as career prospects were concerned. I needed to learn to read and write, to put my thoughts in order and to become more disciplined in my thinking. There was nothing good where I was, only evil. The only refuge in that house was my corner where I could copy out words from comics. I had spent hours doing just that. As I approached my fifteenth year I knew that a greater world was calling me, and I felt ill-equipped to step into it.

Bartley Green was changing. Bulldozers cleared the surrounding farms and new houses were built to accommodate thousands of families. A huge council estate covered the green grass. By the time the development was completed there were ten thousand houses sprawled across the farmland which we had enjoyed playing in. Even after long-term tenants were allowed to buy their homes from the council, nearly

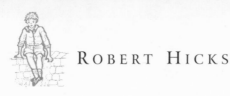

fifty per cent of the huge estate was still rented by low-income residents by the end of the millennium.

The farmer ploughing the fields with his strong horses had long gone. Even the modern tractors and farm machinery that had made the horses redundant had been erased from the landscape. The old oak, whose heart had been ripped out by lightning, was felled without any consideration for its history and the imagination of countless children. It was burnt to ashes within a matter of hours – a funeral without mourners.

254

Our old blacksmith at the forge was the last of his line. Some fortunate family converted the shell of his property into comfortable living accommodation with all mod cons. The blacksmith's glowing face and his blazing fire, which had comforted us children on our cold journey home from school, were consigned to memory. I wondered if he ever knew that his big smile and warm welcome were in themselves little miracles to children like me, who had no smiles and little warmth in their homes. The church of Saint Michael and All Angels fell victim to the redevelopment and so did Miss Treadwell's happy primary school of so many memories. A bland block of flats rose high into the sky in their place. I don't

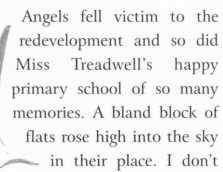

think new residents ever experienced the community spirit that had been the life force of that same plot just a few years earlier. Even the mystical water from the spring that was born at the dawn of creation (according to the legend!) was channelled away by 'progress' so that property could be built above and around it.

Soon the clay pits disappeared and the beautiful trees that had proudly graced the verges of Stonehouse Lane made way for a wide road to accommodate the tens of thousands of cars which sped back and forth. There were no more fetes at Birmetals. You could no longer see the Clent Hills across the fields. The outlook in every direction was changing.

> "The water was cool and clean and according to the teacher it had been running since the moment God made the world. That is a very very long time. It was here before any trees or bushes. Yet it is still here now and I can wash my face in its water and drink it too.
> I wish I could drink it every day."
> — A Child's Thoughts

255

I too was changing. I felt it deep inside my soul. I did not know how the change was taking place but the future looked as dark and black as the past.

Here I was in the house of horror where mother and father had so miserably failed us children. The house held gruesome dark secrets, none worse than the horror of Jean's violation by her own father which led her to believe that suicide was her only option.

Every part of me that had been abused was crying out, not for vengeance, but simply to escape from the house. Not to escape to something I could see, or into the arms of another person as mother had done, but from being destroyed in the future as I had been in the past. I must fight. I must fight my father and not allow the abuse to go on any more. I must take control.

I was strong for my size and years but at home I felt weak and helpless. In two years I grew ten inches, but this spurt of physical growth didn't happen until I had seized my freedom and accepted responsibility for my own future. Dad's brutality and drunken bullying stunted everything. For months I had been saying to myself, 'I will fight. I will fight. I will fight'. Now I decided, 'Tonight I will fight. I will do it!'

Maybe it was because I had witnessed Brian's bruised and battered leg, or because Mr Humphries the headmaster had recently looked me in the eye and told me that I was a failure and had wasted my opportunities, or because there was a big world out

> "I am afraid. I am alone. Soon I will have to find a job and look after myself. But first, there is Dad. I have to face my deepest fear... I have to face Dad."
>
> — A Child's Thoughts

256

there and I knew I could not continue running away into open fields. Whatever the reason, I was determined. I knew that unless I fought back, I would never have confidence for the future.

I was alone in the house. My sister and brothers were in institutions or in care. I can't remember where John was but he may have been working at the Hippodrome in the city centre. I was all alone expecting that Dad would come back in the early hours of the morning as usual. I had worked part of the evening at my cupboard over the gas meter by candlelight. When the gas ran out I used candles. Whatever time I went to bed I made sure I kept my socks and shirt on, ready for when Dad would call me downstairs.

In my dark cold bedroom my mind turned over many memories. I began to cry real tears. Apart from the tears shed in the catalogue lady's house when Dad had insisted I gave him my hard-earned money, I cannot recollect ever crying. My whole family had been bruised and battered. Even Lassie the dog had been mercifully put down. Here on the bed, Ginger the stray cat had given birth to kittens. They'd been drowned the next day in a bucket of water because there would be no food

for them. Ginger kept looking for her kittens and couldn't be consoled until she was pregnant again, and so the cycle continued. It was here in this room that five of us had slept together in the winter to keep warm.

The headlights of the number 12 bus shone through the curtainless window and were reflected on the ceiling. Dad might be on this bus! It stopped. Then, as the bus moved off, the beams glided slowly round the room making it appear as if the bed itself was moving. All was pitch black again. I waited and listened to see if Dad had arrived.

This was the house I had cleaned for him. I had washed his shirts, ironed his clothes and tried to wash the bed sheets. Bernard and Brian would hold one end of each sheet while I twisted from the other end in a vain attempt to wring out the water. This was the house where I made a mutton stew every Wednesday. I boiled the mutton in water and let it cool down so that I could remove the thick slab of fat from the surface. Some of the fat left was used to make dumplings. By adding vegetables and water each day the stew would last until Saturday. This was the house that never heard laughter when Mom and Dad were at home, nor any expressions of love or joy.

As I dwelt on all these memories my mind was flooded by heart-rending images. But I had reached my

decision. By allowing the tears to flow I released the tension within me so I could fight for my future.

The door banged! Dad was home! The moment had come!

At first it was quiet but I knew what he was doing. He was putting some coins into the empty gas meter, then he would light the gas oven, lift up his shirt and warm his backside against its open door. That was when he would call me. 'Bobby, I know you are not asleep. Come down and have a bacon sandwich with me.'

> "I only have one place at 335 that I can call my own: my corner in the living room. The small cupboard box that covers the gas meter belongs to me."
>
> — A Child's Thoughts

That was how it always started – an invitation to share some food or a have a cup of tea. I kept quiet. If I pretended to be asleep and put a peg in the door bolt, he would often have his supper, flop into bed and not wake until noon the following day.

'Come on Bobby. Come down. I know you're not asleep. Come down.'

The tone of his voice was changing. I knew it was one of those nights when he would not take no for an answer, and if he had to come up the stairs to me it would be a very bad night indeed. I called out that I was coming down. I put on the rest of my clothes

259

quickly – short trousers and shoes. The shoes were canvas plimsolls and there was a hole in one of them. Dad's bedroom was opposite mine. The door was open. Dreadful things had happened to Jean in that bedroom and it was where we had planned to put an end to Dad by gassing him while he was asleep. I know now that it would never have worked. The room was too draughty for such a plan to succeed. I walked past Jean's small room which she had kept so tidy and where she used to read the moving story of *Her Benny* to me and my younger brothers. At the top of the stairs was the cold bathroom. We seldom used the washbasin, preferring to wash in the kitchen sink for the kitchen was warmer.

I came down the bare wooden stairs which had not seen a coat of paint for years. I remembered the strange smell when we had opened the front door of the house the very first time. It came from the hastily applied emulsion paint. At the bottom of the stairs on the right was the room where Betty plied her trade as a prostitute while Dad was in prison. Dad must have felt very foolish finding he had lost his money and his girlfriend too. As I turned at the foot of the stairs I passed the all-

> "I know I must fight Dad, but everything inside me is telling me that it's wrong.
> But I can't help it, I must fight Dad."
>
> — A Child's Thoughts

purpose room, where Dad kept his belt and I had my corner. My brothers and I had cleaned and polished the room countless times in order to convince people from the authorities that dad was a caring parent. At the end of the passageway to the kitchen I turned left into the small toilet. On other occasions when Dad violently abused me I regretted not relieving myself first.

'Bobby! Why do I always have to be kept waiting?'

I entered the kitchen. The oven had warmed it up. Every time Dad left the house the gas would run out, yet as soon as he returned he would always find money for the meter so as to keep himself warm. He offered me a bacon sandwich but I refused it. I had learnt a long time ago not to deprive Dad of his bacon.

'Have a cup of tea then.' I poured two cups of tea or rather two jam-jars of tea. The two or three cups in the house were kept for visitors and we were forbidden to use them. I had learnt to put the milk in first so that the boiling tea didn't crack the glass. We warmed our hands on the hot jars but could not hold them for long without burning our fingers.

'Have you got yourself a job, then?'

I told Dad I was going for an interview as an errand boy and there was a possibility of serving an apprenticeship in due course after being assessed. I was keen to do the apprenticeship even though it meant taking a reduction in salary. It offered me an education, something I desperately needed having been a failure at school. Dad asked how much money I would earn and I told him it would be two pounds, sixteen shillings and a penny a week.

Dad exploded! 'Why have I been keeping you all these years if all you are worth is two pounds, sixteen shillings and one penny? You needn't think I am going to keep you any longer! You have bled me dry! Why can't you get yourself a decent job?'

I hadn't expected Dad to talk like this. His ranting confused me. I had been building up for a fight but he had not talked about Mom. He had changed tactics and talked about me and my job.

'You'll have to give me two pounds and fifteen shillings,' he said, 'and think yourself lucky at that.'

That would leave me one shilling and one penny to clothe myself, feed myself at lunch-time and pay my fares to and from work. I couldn't believe it. How could he take so much money from me? I told him I would need money for fares.

'You can walk to work, like I walk to work!' he said.

> "Dad's always saying that Donald and our half-sister Tracey are 'bastards' but he treats us all the same. To him, we are all bastards."
>
> — A Child's Thoughts

262

THE FIGHT

When I mentioned clothes he snapped back, 'What is wrong with the NSPCC? They will always have some clothes for you if you want them. All you have got to do is get off your backside and go and see them.'

And so the late night conversation continued, while Dad ate his greasy bacon sandwiches and drank a second jar of tea. Mom came into the conversation. It was going to end in a fight.

He launched into a monologue. 'Donald is a bastard. That girl she gave away was a bastard. That is the kind of mother you had. She would not even keep her own child. Brian was a bastard too. Any more children she has got now are bastards.'

Then came the questions. 'Have you seen Mr Palmer? Have you seen your mother? You know where she is, don't you? You were the one who called the police, weren't you? Why did you do that? Why weren't you on my side? I was in the right, wasn't I ? She was going off with a black man, like I said and you called the police. You could have stopped but no you had to go and call the police. You were on her side, weren't you, even though she was wrong and all the time she was plotting to leave!'

I was wearing the one thing he had ever given me – the yellow shirt. 'I bought you that shirt. What did she ever buy you?'

> "For five years, I never told Dad about Mom and the strange man on the coach. For five years, I kept a dark secret."
>
> — A Child's Thoughts

As he ranted on, his voice changed, his eyes glazed over and his body twitched. Soon he would turn. I had to be ready for it. I knew it would not be long before he started on about the trip to Bellevue, the day I had witnessed the affection between Mom and Ken Palmer. But I had never told anyone, least of all Dad, what I had seen that day and I certainly wasn't going to tell him now. He was ranting and raving. He wanted to know whether Mom and Mr Palmer had been together at all that day. He could not believe that they could go on the same outing without making contact, and of course he was right.

If I had hinted at the truth five years earlier I know life would have been even more hellish. The person who was glaring at me was no longer my father, but a monster. For the first time I realised that he was not seeing me as his son. He had not looked at me as his son at any time during the nine or ten years that I had called this house my home. I had never been a child whom he could influence for good or into whom he could instil any ambition for a better life, but that night his brain was not functioning properly. He wanted to lash out. He wanted someone to vent his anger on.

THE FIGHT

I did not know what he had done to Jean at that time. If I had known I am sure it would have pumped up my strength and courage to even greater heights. As he came towards me I punched him in the belly with all the strength that I possessed. He doubled over in pain and our eyes met. I saw his fear. I jerked my knee upwards and made contact with his jaw. He bit his tongue and the lower lip sent red blood spurting onto my yellow shirt. His only gift to me was stained with his own blood which I had spilt. He collapsed onto the floor.

Some years later I was trying to help a young man who was heavily into drugs. He described to me how he had killed his father with a bread knife in an attempt to protect his mother. He was convicted of manslaughter, sent to prison and had come out a drug–addict. I recalled the scene with Dad lying on the floor. I could easily have picked up the carving knife which lay on the draining board, or the pan of boiling water from the hob, and used them to inflict more damage on Dad or even kill him. Like this young man I could have gone to prison and come out an addict. Dad was defeated. I was no longer afraid.

I did not want to fight any more but I had to find somewhere safe while Dad calmed down. I jumped over his body, ran into the cold pantry at the end of the kitchen, shut the door and wedged the mop and broom handles against the inner latch so that Dad could not get in. At first there was silence. After what seemed a very long time I heard the tap running. Dad was probably rinsing out his mouth. He had lost two teeth and his mouth had been bleeding profusely.

> "I looked through my Dad's eyes into his soul and it was not nice. He was a 'nobody' and he knew it. His life had turned into nothing and I was ashamed and also afraid, not for his life, but for mine."
>
> — A Child's Thoughts

The pantry was extremely cold, especially the marble slab. Looking at that slab reminded me of the time Dad and Taffy went into the fields hunting rabbits. They smoked them out of their burrows, then killed them with a blow to the back of their necks. Dad would skin the rabbits and they would end up in a stew. Any surplus rabbits were hung in the pantry where I was hiding. As I crouched there I remembered one white rabbit whose neck had not been broken, though it was severely stunned. It had revived in the night and made a high-pitched screeching noise which frightened us all. Dad eventually got up and released it from the pantry where it had been running wild among the corpses of the other rabbits.

THE FIGHT

I was not frightened any more. I might have to fight Dad again but I believed that cowards always back down when someone stands up to them. Nevertheless I looked around the pantry for something I could use as a weapon to protect myself.

Dad came to the door of the pantry. 'Bobby, come out. You have proved yourself a man. We can be friends now. It is all over. I am not going to hit you. Come out. Come on out.'

His tone had changed but I was not going to tempt fate. I told him I would stop in the pantry all night if I had to. He should go to bed. We talked for some time until I felt certain that I had really won. I opened the door and we looked at each other.

He was making a cup of tea. For a moment I was afraid he was going to throw the hot water in my face. My muscles contracted as I prepared to defend myself. Dad wouldn't look me in the eye then or for a long time to come. I do not think he even looked me in the eye when he was on his deathbed, riddled with cancer in his early fifties.

'We can be the best of friends,' he started saying, 'now that you have stood up to me.' I knew that was not true. I had seen other bullies doing exactly the same. The moment someone stood up to them they would change tactics and pretend they had finished with violence, yet they would still try to keep you under their control while they walked away to find other victims.

After a jar of tea, we went to bed. It was the same cold dreadful house, yet it was not the same! I was determined I would never suffer violence again from my father and, for that matter, never again would I be bullied. Whatever my future might hold, I had fought and won a decisive battle. It had only taken a few moments but there were five years of hurt behind those few moments and before me lay a whole new future. I was free from the prison my father had created for me but I still had to break free from the prison of my trapped mind and impossible speech.

> "I am no longer a child. I am now a grown up boy, but I hate the way I became one! I have Dad's blood on my yellow shirt and I know I will never forget this. I have no love in my heart for Dad or Mom and I don't really know my brothers and sister. I am now a grown up boy, but what shall I do with my life. What I do know is that I must not become like Dad."
>
> — A Child's Thoughts

From being an errand boy I became an apprentice, learning the trade of a master grocer. I progressed to become a Manager, an Area Manager, then Marketing Director of retailing, responsible for opening the first

hypermarket/ superstore in the UK. Through my new-found love of literature and books, I changed careers and eventually became Marketing Director for a publishing company, following which I set up my own publishing enterprise, creating a range of publishing companies which years later my sons took over. The companies have offices in different parts of the world and have generated tens of millions of pounds over the years.

Along the way I married and was blessed with four children, though there came a time when we had to fight cancer, not only for my dear wife and other members of the family, but also other cancer sufferers whom we 'adopted' and cared for. I had to drink the cup of bereavement many times. Then I experienced the joy of remarriage and the priceless gift of another little daughter in later life.

These years that lay ahead would bring the rewards, not only of having my own children, but also of fostering children with my first wife, Joyce, and giving them the love and care I was deprived of, and seeing some of those foster children adopted by loving parents.

These years would also bring me into close contact with all classes of people – the so-called 'elite' as well as many middle-class people, whilst never losing the friendship and closeness of poor and working-class folk

ROBERT HICKS

> "As a child, I cried, but no-one heard me cry.
>
> No-one knew the loneliness, the sense of nothingness that comes by being betrayed by one's own parents.
>
> The tears are deep, so deep that I sometimes forget until suddenly they are awakened and I find myself wanting to cry all over again.
>
> I want the pain to go away.
>
> One day, I will laugh... but first I have to learn to speak.
>
> I must learn to speak.
> I must learn to read.
> I must learn to live.
> I must learn to be me!"
>
> ———— A Child's Thoughts

and those below the poor on the invisible social ladder.

Little did I realise that night in the kitchen that I would travel to all four corners of the earth and would see and feel things that I could not possibly have even imagined. The life that lay before me would be a struggle. It would be hard, and there would be many obstacles to overcome, but never, never again would I be bullied

I had come into the world when the bombs were falling. Fifteen years later I had fought for my personal freedom and won. At the end of *Gone with the Wind* Scarlet O'Hara says, 'Tomorrow is another day.'

I had fought for my tomorrows and although I was ill-equipped in every department of my life to make a go of it, I accepted responsibility for my own destiny and my

own future.

No longer a child, I would not bring in extra Family Allowance or dole money. Instead Dad tried to extract every last penny from my earnings week by week. I would have to learn the art of negotiation and compromise, something that came amazingly easy to me.

I was only fifteen years old and small in stature but I was growing up fast. However, I needed a miracle if I was to overcome the problems of speaking, reading and writing as I entered into the new big world of tomorrow. An unbelievable miracle did happen. It set in motion a chain of events which transformed my life beyond recognition, so that within a few years the child from the slums became the boy who spoke with his head held high, who faced the world and did not look back, until the time came when he could write the story of his life! Yes – that is another story!

I needed a miracle and the miracle came … in the person of a divorced nurse who was working in a grocer's shop, and in the person of a surgeon who operated on my tongue then motivated me towards self-education.

I needed a miracle and it came … in the form of a 350-year-old Book of over 1,300 pages, which I was to copy out by hand. It became my education and a door to my future.

Yes, I needed miracle and it came … again and

again ... until one day I would be visiting Buckingham Palace to present a special gift for Her Majesty Queen Elizabeth II during the celebrations of her Golden Jubilee. The gift was a new edition of the same 350-year-old Book that I had copied out 45 years earlier; the same Book, but completely re-designed and re-typeset. The Book upon which Her Majesty had made her solemn vows amid the great drama of her coronation.

CHAPTER 11

HELL REVISITED

'Hell Revisited' was written after
the book 'A Child Cries' was
completed. Although brief, it
became very important to my
sister and me.

Occasionally, when rambling among the fields of the derelict farms in one of my 'run away from it all' moods, I would try to push over any large boulder that I came across.

There was one boulder in particular that I had no success with until I was in my early teens, and even then I only managed to move it partially. I could never topple it over completely.

I was fascinated by the creepy crawlies which lived in the dark and came in many shapes and sizes. I didn't have time to analyse them in detail because as soon as the light penetrated their dark world they disappeared as fast as a rabbit down a hole when it is chased by a fox!

> "I have two fears to
> live with:
> The fear of my father.
> The fear of knowing what
> my father did to
> my sister.
> This second fear has
> become the
> creepy-crawlie that
> I cannot face.
> So I hide it. I hide it
> in the dark."
>
> — A Child's Thoughts

Creepy crawlies living their lives in the dark would be an apt description for so much that went on in the place we called home. One of those creepy crawlies has lived with me all of my life and only now am I making an effort not to run away from the light. It concerns Dad's bedroom and my sister Jean.

After an absence of over forty years I have revisited 335 on four occasions, but each time a cold sweat has prevented me from going into Dad's room.

On my last visit to the old house, I was in the boys' bedroom answering questions to camera for a video. We left that room, which is opposite Dad's room and the door was slightly ajar so I could not help but see inside. That glimpse vividly brought back the details of the room. 335 had one medium-sized bedroom where the five of us boys slept – always in the dark. There were two other smaller rooms. Jean's room, which she had very much made her own, was to the left of the boys' room and Dad's room was immediately opposite our bedroom. Unfortunately even though our room came between Jean's door and Dad's door that did not prevent Dad repeatedly raping Jean in her early teens.

Dad's room was scary. It had a bare wooden floor and the small double bed filled most of the room. There may have been sufficient space for a narrow cupboard and wardrobe but the bed was the sole piece of furniture. The only other item was a chamber-pot

kept under the bed. We never had potties in our room. If nature called in the night we had to make our way downstairs in the dark to the toilet opposite the kitchen door.

Dad's door was never locked. It had a simple latch like all the bedroom doors. Except for a two-inch border of colourful wallpaper about 12 inches from the top of the walls, the rest of the plaster was painted with the council's cheap emulsion paint. Bad workmanship meant that this had dried patchy. The window looked over the front garden and beyond the extended green verge on to the narrow road where the double-decker buses were forced to stop if a vehicle approached in the opposite direction.

I avoided Dad's bedroom like the plague and can remember being in the room only a few times. I slept in that bed just twice – when I first arrived at the house having been taken away from the security and comfort of Erdington Cottage Homes and when Dad was in prison, leaving us in the care of a prostitute from Cardiff.

The only other time I visited that room was to deliver the *Daily Mirror* to Dad before I went to school.

The creepy crawly that has lived inside me in the shadows concerns my cowardice which I kept hidden all my life until I started writing my story. My sense of shame is increased when I recall that while Jean was

ROBERT HICKS

with Dad in the bedroom, I was grateful for the respite from the torment and bullying that would otherwise have come my way in the kitchen. It may seem strange that I have gone through my entire life locking this dark secret away in the depth of my being, never wanting it to come to light and never wanting to admit that I knew what was taking place.

People who have known me for many years will not identify cowardice as one of the flaws in my make-up but I was a coward and deep inside my being I have hidden it away. Time has made the boulder heavier and larger and therefore more difficult to push over to let the light in. Having let the light in, the first person I needed to talk to, and apologise to, was my dear sister, Jean. Jean was relieved that we could talk over those dreadful times and sinful acts that took place a few feet away from my bedroom. She was relieved – but not because she had hidden it away. She had told her children at an appropriate time and their love for her had not been diminished but increased. They respect her for what she has had to overcome. As we talked about the events together, I was even more appalled by what had happened.

My sister attempted to commit suicide on more than one occasion because of the repeated rape and the fear Dad instilled into her. She believed that he would kill her if she breathed a word to anyone. Jean forgave

278

me for acting like the innocent bystander ignorant of what was taking place. With her natural common-sense approach to those past days she reminded me, 'We were but kids. What could we do about it?'

Of course, she is right. But the creepy crawly in my life tried to pretend it never happened by burying it and never referring to it for over forty-five years and never giving Jean any comfort during that time.

> "What happens
> in the dark
> would never happen
> if there was no dark.
> What happens in the
> night would not happen if
> there was no night.
> I must not let the dark or
> the night live inside me,
> otherwise I will become a
> creepy crawlie."
> — A Child's Thoughts

279

I have to leave it to others to draw their own conclusions from all this but I am relieved that at long last the heavy stone has been lifted and even more relieved that the creepy crawly within me has been exposed.

I have chosen my words carefully in writing of the great wickedness that was done to my sister so that the graphics of the evil deeds are not portrayed. It is wise not to display sexual crimes in public, whether in words or pictures, because they only feed the creepy crawlies that remain in the dark rather than generating life in the light.

CHAPTER 12
THE FUTURE

CHAPTER 12

THE FUTURE

When Mr. Humphries, the headmaster of Ilmington Secondary Modern School handed me my School Leaving Certificate, he shook his head and said sadly words to the effect of, 'What a waste!'

I never fully understood what made him say that or what he actually meant. Did he mean that my past was a waste or that my parents were a waste or that I had not reached my potential? He was aware that I had a sharp and analytical mind. Maybe he had read my school reports and seen again and again 'Failed' and was thinking of my future. I had excelled only

"How can the future be a waste before the future has started?
My past – Yes.
My education so far – Yes.
But not my future!
No-one should say my future is a waste!
Now, I am free.
Now, I am responsible.
I can decide for myself whether I waste my future or not.
Today and tomorrow are mine .. not to waste.
Each day I will do what I can and build on that."

— A Child's Thoughts

in Maths. Yes, excelled! But because I played truant for so much of the time including when the exams were held maybe I was deemed to have failed in that subject too.

Whatever the headmaster meant it hurt me for years. In fact, it still hurts! Words can be cruel and I had to fight constantly against the effect those words had on my confidence and to a lesser extent still do.

No-one wants to be a waste yet that was what I felt I was as I looked into the future.

I was uneducated, couldn't communicate properly, unable to read or write, dressed in school clothes that really were rags, without proper shoes but only plimsolls tied up with string on my feet. I didn't have a pair of long trousers and the only decent shirt I had was that yellow one. The NSPCC had provided me with a sleeveless pullover, an old jacket and a plastic mackintosh. I had no money and would have to walk to attend any interviews for work.

My father never physically hurt me again but he harassed me about finding a job quickly because he was no longer receiving Family Allowance for me. Over the next few years he kept on at me to leave home for good. There were many struggles with Dad ahead of me.

So as a small boy in my fifteenth year I looked into the future with no one to help or encourage me and the

future looked dark. Although I was full of fear and confusion I knew there was only one direction to go and that was into the great unknown.

I didn't realise at that time that when I accepted the meanest of jobs as an errand boy for George Mason, the Midlands Family Grocer, it would lead to my problem of being tongue-tied being diagnosed and successfully corrected by surgery which gave me the desire to improve educationally and socially.

Little did I anticipate that the surgeon would place the idea in my mind that I could copy out words from a book to gain a basic knowledge of the alphabet and that this would lead to me copying out a 350 year old translation of the Holy Bible over a period of two to three years.

I did not know then that this would instil in me a love for literature and learning so that over the next few years I would make up for the lack of education which my home life and physical handicap had inflicted upon me.

I had no perception then that by copying out the Holy Bible I would overcome aspects of being dyslexic though I didn't realise that was my problem until I watched one of Esther Rantzen's television programmes about dyslexia. Her guests, Jackie Stewart the racing driver and Susan Hampshire the actress, both suffer from dyslexia.

By educating myself I gained an apprenticeship to become a master grocer. I climbed the promotion ladder over the next fifteen years and took an active part in the retail revolution that began in England during the fifties and sixties.

Eventually I would become the Marketing Director of the largest retail operation in north-west England, with over one hundred shops under my control, as well as being responsible to my Chief Executive for opening the largest out-of-town superstore in the UK at that time.

I could not foresee what the future held and how I would meet and marry Joyce Robinson and have four children, two boys and two girls, all of whom are now married with their own families.

How I struggled to become a husband and a parent, a provider and a mentor, living in constant fear that my father's influence on me would affect my family is a book in itself. There were mistakes in abundance but a great deal of joy as well.

I could not see then that Joyce would be diagnosed with a malignant melanoma cancer after the arrival of our fourth child, or that sixteen years later after numerous operations for the removal of more tumours than any individual should have to bear, the fight was over and she went to Heaven while I was left to try and make sense of it all.

THE FUTURE

If anybody had told me when I was that young boy with nothing, and apparently going nowhere, that my headmaster's prophecy would not come true and that, following a career in retailing, I would turn to publishing and become responsible for thousands of titles and millions upon millions of books and visit Buckingham Palace with my second wife Annabelle and our delightful young daughter Emily-Rose in order to present a Jubilee Bible for Her Majesty the Queen – a new edition of the same Bible which I had copied out by hand 45 years earlier – I would not have believed it to be possible.

But then with an evil path still close to me yet behind me, an unknown future lay ahead. Something inside me told me that the days of a child crying inwardly would give way to the weeks of a boy who would begin speaking and, one day, to the months and years of a man who would learn how to laugh.

Yes there would be a future. But that's another story!

DAD

Dad died of cancer in his early fifties with no friends and nothing he could call his own, not even the love and respect of his children. One of his sons, whose identity will be revealed in my next book, smacked Dad across the face when he was totally helpless and

on his deathbed saying, 'Now you know what it is like to be hit when you are totally helpless like I was as a child!' No doubt you find his action repulsive, which I can readily understand, but this same son cleaned his Dad's bed and washed him during those final weeks. What a mixture of deep emotions he must have been feeling! Two weeks before Dad died I was with my sister Jean in the bedroom of gloom with the realisation that death was near. Dad recognised Jean but was not aware that I was in the room too. As he feebly put his hand out to Jean and said, 'I love you' he accidentally touched her breast and added, 'Not in that way. Not in that way!' I was witnessing a confession of sorts of a great evil that still lingered in Dad's conscience. That greater sin blinded him to the needs of his sons who also had been sinned against, yet no plea for forgiveness came their way and they saw no signs of remorse. There is more I would like to say about the weeks just before Dad died. The opportunity will come my way later.

MOM

Many years after Dad died, and twenty-eight years after she had abandoned her children, fully knowing how they would suffer, Mom reappeared on the scene. It was six months after her partner had died. I am sure that if he had outlived her we would never have heard

from her again and her story would have remained a mystery. But my mother did return, bringing a multitude of emotional pains to her natural children so that they suffered twice. More about my mother in my next book.

THE TWINS

If my research is right, twins were born to my mother in her teens. None of my family has ever met them. My prayer is that they found security with their adoptive parents and that those parents laid a foundation of love and encouragement, so that when the time came for them to establish their own families, it would have been as normal and happy as ours should have been.

DONALD

My eldest half-brother, whom I remember clearly from my childhood though I hardly saw him, was devastated when after twenty-eight years his mother returned. Mom had promised Donald that she would never leave him with his stepfather who had so cruelly and frequently beaten him. Not only did she leave him but she never communicated with him – not even a birthday or Christmas card. After spending an unjustifiable time in Borstal he joined the army where he rose to the rank of sergeant. He met and married

Janice and they raised their happy family in Devizes. Janice believes that the shock of his mother's unexpected return was the cause of Donald's subsequent ill health. He lost the sight in one eye totally and partially in the other and had his foot amputated. He had developed diabetes and when he was hospitalised near me I got to know him and we enjoyed each other's company. Not long after my first wife died, Donald suffered a severe heart attack and my tears at his funeral were heartfelt, even though we had only grown to know each other in the final few years. Donald had very firm convictions, including political ones, and he was a proud and independent individual. I was immensely proud of him, as I am of all my brothers and sister.

JOHN

John (or Jack) was the clever, handsome one with a range of gifts and abilities. I imagined that he had left school with good qualifications. As I began to write my story, John told me that was not the case. Like me he left school with no qualifications. With hindsight, I realised that he struggled with the home situation and spending time in institutions, but he also suffered severely from asthma which required hospitalisation and periods abroad to recuperate. He didn't really have the chance of a proper education. However, his charm,

alert mind and good looks meant he was always employed. He married Pam and they raised children together but sadly later divorced. Fifteen years after the divorce he found new love and happiness and a second marriage with a widowed lady called Margaret. I wish them many happy years together.

JEAN

Her life is a story in itself. Being the only girl in the family, with a father who robbed her of so much, she had gigantic mountains to overcome. She herself admits that she has stumbled many times under the exertion and strain. Jean became pregnant in her teens but the child's father deserted her. When she was pregnant for the third time, her husband George tragically died. Later she nursed a companion through sickness until he too died. Except for her first child, all her children are mixed-race and very proud of their mother. Jean brought up her own children, mainly single-handed, and with unbelievable dramas along the way. She has come through it all marvellously. She has proved beyond doubt that she has nothing to be ashamed of. I will be giving an entire chapter to Jean in my next book, but let me say now that she is a sister of whom I am immensely proud.

292

BERNARD

My younger brother, Bernard has in recent years become a real friend. Like John he suffered from asthma and like Jean he had a squint in his eye which was not remedied until he was twenty-one. In many ways he is the quietest member of the family and in build more like his slim Uncle Tom than our mother. Bernard married Sue and they had two children. Sadly their marriage ended in divorce although I have never heard Bernard make a single criticism of his former wife. Bernard has also come through various crises in his life. For a time he shared his home with a lady whom he married in the hospital just a few days before she died.

BRIAN

My younger brother, Brian, never really had a chance. His earliest memories are of being bullied and knocked about and not having a mother. His schooling was minimal and even today he cannot read or write properly. He had two children with his partner. Brian repeatedly tells me that he sees himself as the black sheep of the family. It is not true but that how he perceives himself. When mother returned he desperately wanted to rekindle a relationship with her. Initially he was willing to put all the blame on Dad and ignore her contribution to the problems at home. If only mother could have been open and honest with

him maybe a relationship could have developed. But she was more concerned with justifying her actions than with accepting her responsibility for those tragic events that caused so much hurt.

HALF-SISTER UNKNOWN

While I am persuaded that one of the reasons mother left was because she was pregnant again by Mr Palmer my research is not conclusive. My Uncle Leslie and my brother Brian have both seen a girl whom they believe to be our half-sister. Although of mixed race she was the spitting image of Jean.

This brings an end to the first volume.

For me, it has been therapeutic and I hope for you, the reader, a reflection of some of the trials and tribulations people have to go through. If you are one of those people, maybe my story is an inspiration for you, proving that it is possible to have the worst start in life, and yet in spite of the handicaps, curses and emotional damage, you can break free from many of them and not transfer them to your own children.

The cycle can be broken.
The cycle must be broken.
Tomorrow's children need all the help we can give them.

ROBERT HICKS

294

"Once I was a child
I thought as a child
I played as a child
I felt as a child
But when I grew up
The child will be no more
I will put away
childish thoughts
I will put away
childish games
But yet the child lives on.
Who I am, is what I was
Who I will be is what
I can be."

A MAN'S THOUGHTS, inspired by
THE APOSTLE PAUL
(1 Corinthians 13, AD 56)

An Appendix

A COLLECTION OF A
CHILD'S THOUGHTS

A COLLECTION OF A CHILD'S THOUGHTS

I was there... when I watched the farmer's huge horses – one white and one black – straining against the leather thongs that pulled the huge cart balanced on two wheels, with its cargo of hay that seemed to reach right up into the sky.

I was there... inside the old oak tree whose heart in an instant had been ripped out by the force of lightning's power, leaving a gash in its side, opening a door for me to enter.

I was there... to drink from a crystal pure spring of cold water whose course had never changed and whose journey had commenced at the birth of the earth.

ROBERT HICKS

I was there... when a huge neglected damson tree, turned wild, produced an abundance of fruit as large as plums, weighing down the strong branches so that I could hide inside as a secret place.

I was there... when the wild wide stream that separated fields flowed freely on its boundless journey to the ocean, and I would pluck up courage to jump across, knowing that – if I failed – my shoes and feet would be soaked and I would laugh aloud for all nature to hear.

I was there... to feel the wind at play, its crazy presence on my face, while my ears tuned in to the melodious sounds of its movements through a myriad leaves on the trees.

I was there... when the bluebells covered the woodland floor so luxuriously and every step I took released a fragrance that filled the air.

I was there... walking along hedgerows older than nations themselves, observing the birds in their nests, touching but never stealing their precious eggs.

I was there... lying on my back, chewing on the stringy lengths of green grass as my imagination made caricatures of the fluffy white clouds moving to and fro.

I was there... climbing proud trees and from a height gazing all around like a young prince surveying his future kingdom.

I was there... when what seemed like ten thousand times ten thousand assembled birds swooped around, filling the skies, preparing for their long journey away from our winter and into warmer climates.

I was there... when cows chewed the green grass and little lambs skipped in the spring and rabbits peered out of their burrows, challenging me to run after them, which I did!

I was there... when the farmer hand-baled his hay in traditional stacks with a 'dolly head' to crown each one, before the machines undertook the task could only produce a standard cuboid brick of hay.

I was there... when there was no artificial light to dim the clear skies at night and the heavens were filled with billions of sparkling eyes, each one winking like a diamond – just for me.

I was there... when the strong horse chestnut tree dropped its seeds, huge shiny conkers encased in spiky protecting balls; conkers through which we could bore holes to thread string for boyish games.

I was there... a child from the slums and there was nothing among the slums and squalor that had prepared me for such a glorious sight and experience.

I was there... aware of the miracle in nature to calm and to heal. It can enrich the soul of anyone who has eyes to see and ears to hear and a heart to respond. I know!... for I was there!

I was there... a child who possessed nothing; a 'nobody' with no adult taking an interest in me. Yet nothing can take away the riches that I enjoyed in the wide expanse of the countryside. Every sense and sensation that had been violated in the slums was revived. Every nerve of the human body regained its sensitivity and eagerly nourished itself in the successive galleries of splendour and glory displayed by the seasons of nature.

I was there... at one with nature, like a baby clinging to his mother's breast.

ROBERT HICKS

302

I was there... like an innocent child learning to crawl, to walk, to run, to dance, to whisper, to speak, to shout!

I was there... in a kingdom fit for any king, the birthright of every child who enters our world.

I was there!

> "I was there!
> All I needed was five
> senses, two feet
> and one heart."
> —— A Child's Thoughts

A ROMANTIC TALE
OF TWO VILLAGES

A ROMANTIC TALE OF TWO VILLAGES

My motive for writing this supplement was originally for the benefit of the two villages where I lived, places that form the backdrop to the events in this book. While this was my initial motivation, as I began to write I realised that there are many city-dwellers who in their moments of reflection, long to spend more time out in the countryside with nature and, if any such city-dwellers become readers of this book, I hope that desire will increase and be translated into action.

A thousand years ago there were two villages at the centre of farming communities that existed next to each other and were barely a dozen miles apart. These two villages were visited by the Norman-French clerks sent out by William the First, known by schoolchildren in England as William the Conqueror to collate national records which later formed the famous Doomsday Book. The Saxon name for one of the villages which would become one of the greatest industrial cities in the world conveyed a picture-story through its three syllables – 'An image of the descendants of a small group or tribe of people making that place its permanent home.' This settlement was called Birm-ing-ham – 'Birm' meaning 'a tribe', 'Ing' meaning 'descendants' and 'Ham' meaning 'residence'. In the Doomsday record its size is given as 480 acres and it had just six ploughs available to till the fields. The financial contribution of Birmingham to the defence of the realm was one English pound.

The name of the second village, which would never be part of the Industrial Revolution was called Berchelar, which simply meant 'a clearing among the birch trees'. Later it took the name that it is known by today – Bartley. As more of the birch trees gave way to farming land, there was a vast area of lush fields, which gave Bartley the additional name 'Green'.

Until the Industrial Revolution these two villages lived side by side with very little evidence of conflict between them, although no doubt a stray cow or a farmer's daughter may have attracted attention and if nature took its course, maybe some tension ensued or affection or something more.

The Industrial Revolution changed everything and within a short period of time the character of both villages altered dramatically. Birmingham became known for its diligent, creative and inventive people and was soon a centre for entrepreneurs who would justify the city's motto, 'Forward'. The communities of

A ROMANTIC TALE
OF TWO VILLAGES

Bartley Green continued to live and work in the way they had done for nearly a thousand years. Birmingham invested in a transport structure that linked it to all major cities throughout the United Kingdom, as well as to the seaports and eventually built an airport too. It recognised the value of waterways and developed a network of canals that could transfer heavy materials swiftly and cheaply through the arteries of the nation.

In contrast, Bartley Green, even before the Industrial Revolution, was finding life difficult to sustain but was not inclined to change. The old men of the farms continued to congregate near the village centre to smoke their pipes and talk, but there were no genuine entrepreneurs to transform Bartley Green in the way that the once-village of Birmingham across the fields was altering beyond recognition from a village to a city. Soon Birmingham boasted shops and department stores, factories and colleges, museums and theatres. By the time silent films became popular, the city was wealthy enough to build picture houses to cater for the ever-increasing audiences the films attracted.

The struggling village of Bartley Green needed the help of the neighbouring town of Northfield to build its first church. The people of Northfield raised the sum of £500 by private subscription for a church that

ROBERT HICKS

barely held 200 people. A school was built opposite the church but initially the children attended irregularly because their families could not survive without their extra labour, especially at busy times in the farming calendar.

Bartley Green sank into such poverty that, prior to the Industrial Revolution, it became a centre for the low paid skill of hand making nails. Bricks were made a few miles outside the village.

The Industrial Revolution provided work for a few men when the third-largest canal tunnel in England, the Lapal Tunnel was built to by-pass Birmingham's city centre. The tunnel left much to be desired. The only way to propel the barges through it was by 'legging' which involved numerous casual labourers lying on their backs on top of a barge and 'walking' along the side walls. It took up to four hours to heave the vessel through approximately 12,000 feet of dingy cavern.

In stark contrast to Bartley Green, Birmingham had become a wealthy city, boasting of quarters for the jewellery trade and benefiting from so much ingenuity that it became known as the City of a Thousand Trades. Birmingham was protected by its variety of trades, unlike other towns which depended on just one or two trades and suffered when they failed. The 'Forward' looking City Fathers created a climate for

308

growth and prosperity that turned Birmingham into one of the major cities of the world and the second most important city in England after London.

Meanwhile Bartley Green, barely a stone's throw away, was unknown and in deep decline, with little work and even less money. Birmingham's city centre was thriving with huge buildings and busy shops all powered by electricity. Bartley Green was still powered by gas with a single exterior gaslight barely illuminating part of the small village.

By the time I moved into Bartley Green in 1946 there were still vast fields and hedgerows. One of those hedgerows was over 800 years old. It was part of Hole Farm at the end of Watery Lane (so called because a stream constantly flowed down its course).

While Birmingham, now recognised throughout the world, was building a new image reflecting the development of its city centre and modern buildings, Bartley Green retained its farms, even though many were left empty. These farms such as Wilderness Farm, Stonehouse Farm, Heathy Farm, Four Dwellings Farm, Broad Hindley Farm, Hole Farm and Lea Place Farm were hundreds of years old. Nonesuch Farm, situated behind our house, perpetuated the legend that Oliver Cromwell had sheltered there when fleeing from the battle of Worcester. When the Cavaliers came searching for him the farmer swore on oath that

'Nonesuch is here'. A lane has been named after Cromwell which feeds the myth but there are no historical records to verify the story.

In common with other great industrial cities, the emerging middle classes of Birmingham demanded a greater infrastructure to preserve their new and prosperous way of life – parks, roads, schools, swimming pools, colleges, museums and art galleries. But there was a terribly dark side to the city that would not go away – the slums that were hastily built at the beginning of the Industrial Revolution to accommodate the tens of thousands of workers drawn to seek their fortune in the Big City. These back-to-back houses provided no sanitation, no running water, no heating, no lighting and very few rooms per family so overcrowding became common. My grandparents and my parents lived in the squalor of the slums and so did I for a few years. It doesn't take much imagination to transport myself back into the misery of childhood in that environment.

The buildings were condemned almost the moment they were built. Crowded together so closely that natural light and air circulation was limited, they were built around small courtyards of cobbled stone, where children like me would kick a tin can for a football, and climb the gas lamp – the nearest substitute to a tree. We seldom went beyond the courtyard where there was very little room for imagination to take root and grow.

Over two hundred thousand people were still living in the slums when Hitler's bombers flew over Birmingham during the Blitz. Between twenty-five to thirty people shared each outside toilet and fifty to sixty people one outside water pump.

In my grandmother's house in the slums the shared courtyard led straight into the small all-purpose room. A large carved cupboard took up most of the space. On top of it was a glass dome protecting stuffed coloured birds. I doubt whether grandmother had ever made a trip beyond the slums in her entire life and her only symbolic contact with the bigger world outside was contained in that glass dome.

What the giant city needed was acres of land for expansion and nearby was Bartley Green which had not embraced the Industrial Revolution and still boasted fields and streams, hedgerows, trees and bluebell woods. Countless houses with front and back gardens and local amenities on the doorstep had been built in the suburbs for Birmingham's middle-class citizens who held voting power, but little had yet been done for the poorest of the poor who had no collective voice. They were an unwelcome presence in the city centre and a genuine problem which presented a health risk that had to be addressed. What the lack of political will could not achieve Hitler's bombs did.

Over 100,000 homes, many among the slums, were destroyed.

Before the bombing, vast areas of central slums had been cleared to make way for the construction of the new magnificent city buildings alongside wide streets. Most of the tenants had nowhere to go and had retreated to the remaining slums in vast quantities.

Efforts had been made after the First World War to cope with the city growth but they were too little and too late. Once the Depression came, the city's wealth was diverted from slum clearance. Soon afterwards preparations for the Second World War and the war itself further delayed these plans.

Hitler's destruction forced a decision on new housing. Something had to be done and Bartley Green came to the rescue with its farms and fields. Over 10,000 municipal houses have been built over the past forty years on land that had been farmed by successive generations for a thousand years.

Fortunately Woodgate Valley at the heart of Bartley Green was preserved although in 1979 it was again in danger of being lost. Wisely local people strongly protested against the planned new development and won. Woodgate Valley has become one of the giant green lungs circulating fresh air not only to the 10,000 municipal houses but to Birmingham itself and its surrounding suburbs. So Bartley Green surrendered its

soul to the desperate needs of Birmingham.

The two villages that once lived side by side depend upon each other in a multitude of ways and allow their people to participate and partake of their combined heritage. Once kept apart they are now united for their mutual benefit.

As I write I have pictures from Bartley Green's history spread before me. There's one of hay-making with two magnificent and powerful horses straining to pull the huge loads of hay piled on a wooden cart. Another picture is of the old forge and wheelwrights shop in Jiggins Lane showing the owner repairing a huge cartwheel while two young girls play in the back yard. A third picture is of the old school, now demolished, and the fire station. You can see the wall of the churchyard with its archway entrance lit by a gas lamp. There is a dirt track road with another gas lamp in the middle of a junction. The signposts point towards Frankley and Northfield. A picture of the bus terminus at Bartley Green includes a bicycle fitted with a canopy to protect it from the weather and an outdoor weighing machine operated by a halfpenny.

In my mind I can walk along the lanes – Adams Hill and Woodgate, Caldhill Road and Cromwell Lane, Field Lane and Scotland Lane, Jenners Lane and Clapgate Lane, Mill Lane and Barnes Hill and of course Stonehouse Lane, which even in 1946 was too narrow for two cars to pass each other without one stopping. Stonehouse Lane is now a wide highway carrying thousands of cars each day with no hint of the long row of trees that once bounded the green verges. I can picture Jiggins Lane. The church and school used to be the village centre. There was a pub called The Cock which I never entered and a little tin Gospel Hall, then further up Jiggins Lane was the forge and right at the top the terminus.

When I left the slums they did not come with me, yet having left Bartley Green, I could not leave it behind. Old Bartley Green is part and parcel of me and although since I left I have travelled to many parts of the world and witnessed many remarkable sights and experiences, none of these has entered my soul like Bartley Green. I had to leave Bartley Green with all its miracles, charm and mystical influence in my formative years, with all its healing power for the daily bruising of body and soul because I had to encounter a future that would test every fibre of my being..

Bartley Green, you have given me a thousand images and experiences, none of which I regret. I am glad that I was there before the city of Birmingham consumed the miracle Bartley Green offered so freely. I watched the farmer's huge horses. I went inside the old oak tree whose heart was ripped out by lightning in an instant. I drank from a crystal pure spring of cold water whose course had never changed and whose journey had commenced at the birth of the earth. I hid inside the branches of the huge neglected damson tree which turned wild and produced an abundance of fruit as large as plums, weighing down the strong branches to form a secret place. I jumped across the wild wide stream that flowed freely on its boundless journey to the ocean. I felt the wind at play on my face, while my ears tuned in to the melodious sounds it made as it moved through a myriad leaves on the trees. I walked through the bluebells which luxuriously covered the woodland floor and every step I took released a fragrance that filled the air. I wandered along hedgerows older than nations themselves, observed the birds in their nests, touched but never stole their precious eggs. I lay on my back chewing on the stringy lengths of green grass as my imagination made caricatures from the fluffy white clouds moving to and fro. I climbed proud trees and from a height gazed all around like a young prince surveying his future kingdom. I watched what seemed like ten thousand times ten thousand assembled birds swoop around, filling the skies, preparing for their long journey away from our winter and into warmer climates. I saw cows chewing the green grass, little lambs skipping in the spring and rabbits peering out of their burrows, challenging me to run after them, which I did! I witnessed the farmer hand-baling his hay in traditional stacks with a 'dolly head' to crown each one, before the machines took over and produced standard blocks of hay. I was there when there was no artificial light to dim the clear skies at night and the heavens were filled with billions of sparkling eyes, each one winking like a diamond – just for me. I collected the seeds of strong horse chestnut trees – huge shiny conkers encased in spiky protecting balls – and chose the ones to thread string through for a game of conkers.

I was a child from the slums and there was nothing among the slums and squalor that had prepared me for such glorious sights and experiences. I was aware of the miracle in nature to calm and to heal. It can enrich the soul of anyone who has eyes to see and ears to hear and a heart to respond. I know for I was there! I was a child who possessed nothing, a nobody in whom no adult took any interest. Yet nothing can take away the riches I enjoyed in that wide expanse of the countryside. Every sense and sensation that had been violated in the slums was revived. Every nerve of the human body regained its sensitivity and eagerly fed on the successive galleries of splendour and glory displayed by the seasons of nature. I was at one with nature, like a baby clinging to his mother's breast. I was there like an innocent child learning to crawl, to walk, to run, to dance, to whisper, to speak, to shout! I was in a kingdom fit for any king, the birthright of every child who enters our world.

> "Nature's beautiful healing properties to body, soul and mind cannot be exaggerated to those whose ears, eyes and heart are open."
> — A Child's Thoughts

Would you like to go down into the fields and woods today? If so, you will be in for a big surprise! If you visit the Midlands, which is at the heart of England, why not go to Woodgate Valley Park? It is still there exhaling fresh air from its huge lungs to the residents of two villages which are now part of one city – Birmingham.